Children Are
Little Mirrors

Children Are Little Mirrors

James Laury Sr.

To order additional copies of this book, contact:
Xlibris Corporation
1-888-795-4274
www.Xlibris.com
Orders@Xlibris.com
33192

CONTENTS

NOTES
ABOUT THE AUTHOR

The Author, James Laury Sr., was born in the City of Philadelphia Pennsylvania during the Civil Rights laden Fifties. There he was exposed to Organized Crime, Civil unrest, Mandatory School Busing, and corruption on every level of Life. Growing up in a multi-cultural neighborhood outside of South Philadelphia, he became very active in the city's Music and Sports scene. Having a Brother, who in his early years, was one of the first Black Dancers on the American Bandstand, James was exposed to some of the top entertainers in American Music. Today, his Brother is a very successful Philadelphia Physician, who counsels James on a frequent basis on proper Health and Nutrition. While learning to survive the very tough streets of Philly, he developed an interest in the study of people around him.

After losing both his Parents at a very early age, he quickly understood the meaning of the Extended Family. He received counsel of many adult mentors from a variety of different walks of Life, from Professional Athletes to retired Educators. During High School, he received an academic scholarship to attend the University of Minnesota. This scholarship was the result of James spending a part of one of his High School years at the exclusive Phillip Exeter Academy, in Exeter New Hampshire, as a part of a Governmental Educational Experiment. At the University of Minnesota, his horizons were immediately broaden, being exposed to classmates from all over the world. Spending much of his free time, sitting and talking with as many Foreign students as would converse with him. Taking every opportunity to visit the homes and families of many classmates.

At the University, James fell in Love with a young L.A. model, who was also attending the School. They began their family during his Senior year. Thus the Family journey began with the birth of their first child (a girl). As he mentions often in this Book, that none of his four children came into this world with Instruction Manuals on what to do with them. Regardless, the Laury Family began with two college kids taking on the role of Parents. As

Parents, they literally knew nothing about Parenting or Childcare. However, as College students, they taught how to research and find sources of information. The Family's Journey started in their college town of Minneapolis, Minnesota and later continued to the City of Seattle, Washington. James began his working career with a Fortune 500 Computer Firm. There he started his employment at the back door and working his way up the corporate ladder to middle management. James turned over the first "No Money Down" Real estate deal to pay for the births of his first two children and a tremendous amount of early Family debts. As soon as his first two children began school, James was transferred to Seattle, Washington. After experiencing many of Family Life's pitfalls (he discusses in the Book) and being a very young Family (without good counsel) and some other unfortunate circumstances. A Divorce occurred which left James to raise his four young children alone, as a single parent. That is the reason, there is a chapter in this book called "Single Parenthood."

One of the sources that he found very helpful, was the advice of Grandmothers. For the Laury Family, every Saturday Night was laundry night at the local Senior Citizens Community Housing Development. James would pack up that weeks dirty laundry and the small kitchen television set, and he and all four children would a Family Night at the Laundry facility. While teaching his children the art of doing laundry. During the week, James would write down questions of that weeks Child encounters. While the clothes were washing, he would discuss his list with the Grandmothers, who also used Saturday night for their laundry. There he received an abundance of wisdom from the Brainstorming Grandmothers, who took great pride in speaking about their experiences of raising children and grandchildren. Solutions to many Family problems were resolved during the Dry cycles.

Even today, James knows that the best resource of information is a conversation with someone who has lived through a situation. There is a wealth of untapped wisdom living among our Senior Communities and our Libraries. James has encountered many of Family's difficulties and he is sharing in this Book "words of wisdom" to help others to avoid some of Life's Pitfalls.

CHAPTER I

CHILDREN

ARE

LITTLE

MIRRORS

CHILDREN ARE LITTLE MIRRORS

Parenting is an area that we all think that we can hide and not face certain facts about children. Those little things known as *GENES* seem to always be working in our children's lives. Children are little mirrors of our outward actions, as well as our personally traits and mannerisms.

Let us begin with our outward actions. It can be as simple as the wrinkling of our forehead or the kringling of the nose in reaction to events. Many times you will observe your child maximizing that facial expression. Yes, just like your mom or dad. We all have many habitual body part movements that we perform regularly. You can bet the family jewels that our children will soon be mimicking those identical movements These movements are usually first noticed by a grandparent or one of your siblings (someone who was with you growing up). They will always notice traits or mannerisms in in your children, traits that you performed as a youth during your childhood. These are mannerisms certain of your *Genes*. You will hear those family members making statements like: "WOW!!!! How did your daughter learn to do that . . . . because that is exactly the way you would do it when you were growing up. Sometimes you will notice your child imitating you or your spouse (partner). Usually the child will imitate the most annoying traits of his or her parents. You will catch yourself saying things like: "You're just like your father, or youre just like your mother!!!" If your child spends much time around the Grandparents, your child will imitate in words and actions the grandparents. If your child goes to Daycare with other Children from different homes. Your child *WILL* bring home different words and actions copied from them.

Now, realizing that your child is going to copy your actions, you as the child's parents can become conscious of the environment that you create for your child to imitate. For example: You can clean-up the *Bad Language* (cursing and swearing) and maybe your *alcohol* and *Drug Consumption*. If not for yourself, than clean-up for your children's sake.

CHAPTER II

TAKE

LOTS

OF

PICTURES

TAKE LOTS OF PICTURES

Time flies when you have children, therefore, take as many pictures as you can when your children are still little. Consider including yourself in the pictures taken with your children because you change along with them. I cannot emphasize the importance of taking pictures; please make yourself to invest in a couple of small handy cameras. I realize that we live in the technology-advanced date of videotaping, but it is still very convenient to grab the little camcorder and toss it into your purse or backpack. Consider even keeping one camera in the family car. You will be surprised the number of times you will be running late for an after school activity such as the Little League Baseball or the Soccer Match and wish that you had a camera to catch the moment of your child's first home-run or a goal. Sale of disposable cameras at after school activities sounds like a great business idea, would not you agree?

It is important to continue taking pictures of your children with yourself. Law enforcement agencies encourage parents to keep current photos of all family members. Capturing the numerous changes of style, opinion, and interests may become a necessary tool should your family experience a communication or a generation gap breakdown. A photograph is a visual-aid, or tracking record, for example, of smiles changing into frowns. If a communication breakdown occurs, the photos will reveal subtle as well as drastic changes in the lifestyle and friendships of your children. As you will examine the changes, the photo will reveal your involvement in your child's life during that time. Perhaps that was the stage when you had to take on more responsibilities at work, resulting in less quality family time together. The pictures may speak loud and clear when the seed of trouble has been sown.

Do not confine picture taking to members of immediate family only. Plan to include grandparents, parents, aunts, and uncles in the pictures with your children. Unfortunately, sickness and death visit every family tree. Trying to explain who the late aunt Susie was would be easier with the visual aid of a photograph. As the old cliche states, "a picture is worth a thousand words." Eventually, as your child will grow older you may start hearing some teenage responses such as: "Dad, mom, that's kid stuff, I don't want my picture taken!!!" or "All right, come on, and hurry up, take that stupid picture." Take the picture anyway! I guarantee it that ten to twelve years from now, you and your children will be enjoying looking through the photo albums together.

Besides, your children will always need pictures for their High School . . . . as well as College Awards ceremonies. Only God knows the future, your child someday may become *famous* in some Political, or some other positive way. Those childhood photos could become priceless. So, just take the picture.

CHAPTER III

A

GOOD

MEDICAL

FOUNDATION

A GOOD MEDICAL FOUNDATION

Before we begin this Chapter, I need to make something perfectly clear. As parents and Team leaders, we must take an honest look at ourselves. We must examine the physical and mental condition of ourselves. The ideas and suggestions in this book will not work at all, if we are unstable or in need of Professional counseling of some kind. For example: If one or both parents are needing Anger Management Counseling or alcohol/ drug Abuse counseling. This book is in *No Way* a substitute for Professional help. Believe me, getting your family off to a good start is of the utmost importance for raising success minded children. So. please Parents, do not allow pride or stubbornness to prevent you from obtaining the Professional supervision that will maximize the potential of your family's future. Recognize that there are professional counselors who can help you with: Depression, Post-Partem syndrome, habits (smoking, drinking, drugs, pornography, sexual perversions), diet (obesity, healthy eating, preparing healthy meals), also different types of Phobias and other self-inflicting phycological situations, etc . . . . There are so many good Physicians, who specialize in those very personal areas of our lives. Every Hospital has these Trained Professionals that specialize in a variety of helpful counseling areas. Remeber, you are not the only person who has ever experienced what you are facing. If you have no Family Doctor, simply go the information center of any major Hospital in your town, and ask to be directed to an administrative person to help you. If the hospital seems to be busy . . . . please just use a little patience with the information people. Remember, the people at these information desks are not Professional people, they are simply volunteers and do not represent the Staff nor the Management of that Hospital. So please, do not take what what they say personally. Their sole purpose is to tell you where you can find the Doctors.

Regardless of how busy the Hospital may seem . . . . *Do Not, Do Not* leave the Hospital without speaking to someone. Many people will use the excuse that they went to the Hospital and it too busy or the information people could not help them. Do not give up!!! Look at the Hospital Directory for the location of the Emergency Room. Go to the Emergency Area Front desk and ask to speak to the Triage Nurse on Duty. Every Emergency Room has a Triage Nurse on Duty (for those Minor non-emergency). The Triage Nurse is a Professionally trained Nurse who has knowledge of many different problems and illnesses. She will direct you to the Professional that can help you.

Establishing a good foundation always begins with the Head (or the top AND WORKS IT WAY DOWN THE CHAIN OF COMMAND. In a Family, starting with the Father and Mother, uncovering any physical or mental problems that may influence the rest of the family. Having a Family Doctor is so important Having a medical Physician who is familiar with the medical conditions of everyone in the family is so vital. Children will be seen by a doctor much more frequently than their parents. However, preventative medical attention more feasible when the Doctor is familiar with any hereditary problems. In other words, if the Doctor is aware of any problems that the parents may have had . . . then he can better treat the children.

Heredity means (transmission) passed down from ancestors to children, if the parents have a medical problem . . . . there is a good chance that the children may have the same problems in their lifetime.

When starting a family, it is so important to seek medical help to take control of any medical situations.

CHAPTER IV

CHILD

PROOFING

THE

HOME

****

THE

FOOT-STOOL

THEORY

CHILDPROOFING

Childproofing happens to be one of the most difficult components of parenting for the reason that it touches the egos of most parents. Many young, stubborn, and rather immature parents are very resistant to the required physical changes or adjustments to their homes. You may hear such remarks as: "Well, I'm going to raise my toddler to respect my valuable thing." Good luck!

Truth is when you invite some of your adult friends over to your place, many of them, after a couple of beers, will begin to disrespect your furniture, rugs, dish-ware, and etc. Can anything more be expected from your precious toddler who really does not recognize the value of your furniture, rugs, and dish-ware? Your child at such an early age is desperately trying to develop a sense of his or her surroundings through sight, touch, and lets not forget taste. Please, do not expect your child to learn what is valuable to you before he or she has even gained the slightest grasp on reality. Allow your child to be a child. Do not be in a great hurry for them to grow up; believe me, they will grow up faster than you will realize. Once again, time really flies with the young ones.

THE FOOT-STOOL THEORY

You, being the parent, wiser and mature, are responsible for the safety of your children. You should operate your household, acknowledging the curiosity and the folly that accompany young age. If you already have young children, I greatly recommend performing a "foot-stool experiment" in every room in your house. While sitting on the footstool in the middle of the room, you place yourself on the eye level of your child. Carefully observe every square inch of the room, from the floor to the ceiling. Rotating your body around on the footstool, you should note any objects that might arouse curiosity of your child; for example, that beautiful glass fruit-bowl you have received as a wedding gift from your family. One day, the playful light on the shinning edge of the bowl will catch the eye of your child. You might feel that you can verbally say "No!" to your child and get the desired results of immediate obedience, but eventually, the child will reach for that shinning edge. Save yourself the future trouble, replace the still-undamaged fruit-bowl with a plastic or a Rubbermaid one, and consider doing the same for other coffee and end table objects. Please, replace that expensive vase or a custom made lamp before either will meet its early unfortunate end. The hanging lamp installed out of child's reach would be as convenient to you, but much safer to the child. The replacement of the fragile vase for something made out of soft wood, cork, or rubber will not be as injurious to your child in case of an accident. Make sure that all materials on your tables are not hazardous to children of all age group, including adult literature. All adult items should be securely stored and locked away, including properly locked up lethal weapons (guns, knife collections, etc.).

The two most difficult areas of the house to childproof are the kitchen and the bathrooms, but both are a necessary must. The process in the bathroom should begin with removing all cleaners, chemicals, and medication out of reach of children. Here I would like to suggest storing all of your personal medication in a cool place in your bedroom. Try to take your medications (prescriptions) in the privacy of your bedroom, out of sight of your children. When grandmas an granddads come to visit, politely ask them to abide by this rule. Keep in mind that your children will mirror the actions of adults, beginning with the search for pills to take to be just like grandmas and granddads. In your child's mind the bathroom might be the place for easy access of pills and cigarettes, so when childproofing, please, remember to remove all ash trays (which will have an additional benefit of making it easier to ask your smoker friends to smoke outside and never around your children).

In the kitchen, the childproofing begins with renewing your mind to remembering to point pot and pan handles to the inside of the stove while cooking. The pot handle will always look attractive to your interested child, especially when curious looking stream is coming out from it. Please, mothers, put away out of reach of your children all of the glassware, china dishes, and the sterling silverware, including the cutlery set holders set on your kitchen countertop. Consider allowing your family to sacrifice four or five years eating out of Rubbermaid plates, plastic tumblers (cups and glasses), and hard rubber utensils. Trust me, this minor adjustment will not distort the flavor of your meals.

No room is ever found without at least one electrical outlet, the most forgetful by parents and the most accessible to children, household component. All electrical outlets should be plugged up by inexpensive plugs found in any hardware store. The plugs, well-worth the investment, will prevent your child from pocking any small object into the open electrical sockets. While not in use, all electrical items, such as wall and floor fans, vacuum cleaner, toaster, waffle maker, and other countertop items, should be unplugged. Remember to close up the outlet as soon as you unplug the electrical item.

With all the above mentioned suggestions of childproofing all of your rooms, your child should be fairly safe in your house, but what about outside?

OUTSIDE RULES AND SUGGESTIONS

Parents, please do not develop a habit of leaving your sleeping unsupervised infant in the car, with the motor running, in any weather condition. I understand the great temptation to let the little one, who has been active and hyper all morning, sleep, while you run the errands. Stop and consider your child's value worth to your family structure and realize that no errand is worth placing your child in danger: 1) kidnapping; 2) waking up and kicking the car in gear; 3) waking up and locking up all the doors; or 4) waking up and coming out of the car to look for you. Do you really need all that extra drama in your life? It would be much safer to befriend your retired neighbors so you can occasionally call on them to baby-sit for you while you run your errands. Besides, the retired couple would probably love to come over and watch their favorite soap operas on your large HD TV.

CHAPTER V

OPEN

COMMUNICATIONS

....WHEN

THEY

ARE

YOUNG

OPEN COMMUNICATION
WHEN THEY ARE YOUNG

When you will grasp the metaphor that your children are tiny mirrors, you will begin to acknowledge the power that you have as a parent to shape and mold many aspects of your child's mannerism. Each child will develop his or her own personality, but his mannerism and social traits will be influenced by you. Your influence will be seen in his respect for others, including authority and elders of the community; personal hygiene; appearance; and other areas. Children are great observers and imitators of their parents' actions. The tone of your voice as you speak to your spouse would affect the manner in which your child will address him or her later in life. The way in which you converse with others will affect your child's future responses. You, as a parent, set this communication tone in your household.

There are many adults who would be defined as introverted. Due to their natural shy personalities, they are not very talkative even within their own families. There is professional counseling available to help these parents overcome their natural shy tendencies as well as address other problematic character traits that might hinder him or her from opening up to the children. These parents must make a decision whether they would like their children to imitate their introverted tendencies even if these traits are not in their child's nature. If you happen to be introverted, I can only imagine how difficult it (might) must be, especially in the beginning, but you must force yourself out of your shell to practice open communication with your children. These children look up to their parents to develop their ways of thinking and communicating, starting at the early stages of their lives.

Open communication is a form of communicating in which you speak to your children and allow them the opportunity to think and respond back to you. This is not a "ga-ga-goo-goo" talk. This is an actual call and response interaction. You must start as soon as the child begins to repeat formed words. Practice allowing them to answer you. Remember to appear interested, making your child's responses seem important to you. Practice this communication with trivial as well as important inquiries. You will be surprised by the ease and openness of your communication with your child as time will pass. With time, you will develop the ability to ask your precious child "who broke that mirror?" in the same sweet tone as asking the little darling how his or her morning happened to be in the kindergarten class. Raising children takes a lot of work and discipline on the part of the parent, having same demands of continuous work and development as in retaining open communication with your spouse.

A family needs a strong foundation on which to build, grow, and nourish. Parents, your unity, or agreement, is that strong pillar on which your family is built. You and your partner must always act in agreement as team leaders. Children have an innate way of detecting a division of opinion among parents. At a very young age, children learn the usefulness and effectiveness of pitting one parent against the other. What I mean is that your child's calculating mind collects data on which parent happens to be more lenient about rules. You may find yourself involved in a conversation to which I refer to as a Ping-Pong effect: "Dad, can I go to . . . . ?" No! Oh, please, Daddy! No! "Mom would let me go!" Then go ask your Mother! "Mom, may I please go to . . . . ?" No! "Oh, Mom, please, dad would let me go to . . . . !" All right, if your Father says you can go, then you can go. "Hey, Dad, mom said that I can go to . . . . !" Well, if your mother said that you can go, I guess, you can go. This happens to be a very common situation in which the child is not trying to be malicious but, nonetheless, shows natural selfish tendencies. It would happen more often in the household where parents are too busy in their own lives to take the time for proper guidance of their children.

Keep in mind that rearing healthy children requires secure, stable (including not moving every time the company expects you to move), peaceful, and loving environment. A word to team leaders: please make a commitment with your spouse for the sake of your children to not fight, or argue loudly, at home in front of the young ones. Even newborn babies can instinctively feel tension, strife, and anger within the family, responding with distressed bouts of crying and wailing.

With the rise of tension within the marriage relationship, parents should take the time out. Have the names of several short notice, preferably teenagers, baby-sitters ready at hand. You may be gone for only a few hours, which would be an excellent time to seek professional marriage counseling. The counseling is to help bring out pent-up feelings that might be too difficult to reveal to each other on your own. There is nothing shameful in seeking professional marriage counseling. Think of a car that periodically needs a tune-up after so many faithful miles. Nothing negative would come from confirmation that parents are traveling down a good road. Believe me, with children in the family there will be many bumps, curves, and twists on the road of life.

If you suppose seeking professional help to be unnecessary, then consider taking a drive with your spouse to an isolated place away from children playgrounds. Being away from home, neighbors, and friends, would be a good time to let out all negative emotions. Air out all those pent-up disagreements; scream out, if you must, to get them off your chest. After the initial screaming, make a decision to come to some permanent or temporary solution before you return back home. The point of these isolated meetings is not to walk away more confused and angry than before, but to come up with a solution.

In the military, and business companies, we occasionally hear of staff meetings at which the leaders of different departments meet to discuss the game plan or the direction the company should take. These leadership type of meetings never occur in front of troops or company workers. Parents, the leaders of the family, should map out a strategy in agreement and only then present it to the children. These meetings should not necessarily be shouting matches in the park; perhaps, it would be more pleasant for the parents to retreat for a love and unity weekend to a ski mountains cottage or maybe a beach hotel away from the troops. Do invite the grandparents to stay the weekend with the children in order to develop a good and healthy relationship between these two generations. After the weekend of planning future family strategies, you then will return to the troops refreshed and ready to lead your family on to a more victorious living.

This book is not a substitution for professional family counseling. Seek out advice or referrals by talking with your clergy or family physician.

CHAPTER VI

WHAT

INFLUENCES

YOUR

HOME

WHAT INFLUENCES YOUR HOME?

Your home is the place where you relax, let your hair down, and be yourself. Many say that home is where the heart is, which leads me to ask, "what's in your home?" What is the main theme or emphasis of the home that you expose your children to? Look around the physical structure within the rooms surrounding your child, and ask yourself, "is this what I want my child to identify with?"

Is your living room full of beer posters or references to alcoholic beverages that your boyfriend, or the child's father, enjoys now or then, or perhaps a bit too often? Or, are the wall of your apartment covered with scandal-clad bikini models sitting atop some commercial product such as a motorcycle or a sports car? Perhaps there are rooms within your home arrayed with nude or sexually explicit posters. If you have a young daughter who is exposed to such images at such an early age, can you really be surprised that during her teenage years she will be dressing very provocatively, or should I say "sleazy," imitating these models? By having such images at your home you are allowing such pictures to be imprinted onto your child's subconscious mind.

What about a young boy who is exposed to sexually explicit photos, be they are calendars, posters, or playboy magazines on the coffee table. You can if you wish forbid the young one to look at the magazines until you turn blue in the face, but what happens when you are not present? The forbidden fruit is too tempting and irresistible. The child will memorize these visual images, arousing appetite for pornography for later in life due to his natural born curiosity gone astray. Perhaps you have not created a monster, but you have helped to shape a womanizer, sexual predator, or maybe even a pedophile. These results are never desired by any parent, but many seemingly harmless influences will contribute to such negative consequences.

Is your home an open doorway for consistent drug- or alcohol-intake traffic? Then realize that it is not a beneficial environment for raising a child. Consider moving your child out of those circumstances. It would be preferable to raise a child in financially poorer but more positive conditions. Do not attempt to raise children where illegal or elicit activities are perceived as part of normal lifestyle. Young children are too innocent and vulnerable to be exposed to such negative influences; if you know of children, living in these potentially dangerous environments, take action. Report it to professionals who can really help that family. Many agencies such as child protective services are equipped to provide help to those children in need.

Many times, families who are crippled by drug or alcohol abuse do not realize the volatility of their situation. Many dysfunctional families do not perceive or refuse to perceive themselves as deviating from the norms. Our present society is too lenient on defining the line between good and bad, right and wrong. Society too freely allows dysfunctional behavior to exist as "diverse preferential lifestyle." Call it anything you wish, but exposing children to illegal activities within their own homes will not lead to anything good. Danger will usually follow an illegal activity; through experience adults have learned how to defend themselves, but what of the vulnerable children?

CHAPTER VII

TIPS

FOR

THE

NEWBORN

IMPORTANT TIPS FOR THE NEWBORN:

Never leave your newborn child alone, except when the child is sleeping. You always want to be within ear (sound) reach of your child . . . just in case of servere coughing or choking. When you are laying your newborn in his crib . . . . always lay the child on his back. Many researchers have found that laying the newborn child on his or her stomach has led to SIDS (Sudden Infant Death Syndrome). Make sure that you do not place sheets or other coverings over the the childs mouth or nose. This could possibly block air flow for the child . . . while sleeping. Always take the time to check that the child's crib has side rails, and that those side rails are up before walking away from your sleeping child. You will be surprised at the amount of movement of your child when sleeping. Also, keep the stuffed animals out of reach while the child sleeps. An innocent stuffed Animal could fall onto the child, by an adult shaking the floor in another room. There is a great temptation to leave the home to run some short erand after you have finally gotten your newborn to sleep, but please leave someone responsible with the child to supervise. Remember, a distracted person is never a good supervisor for your little one. For example: Uncle Joe, who is watching an important Baseball Game in your living room, is probably going to have the volume on the television so loud that he may not hear the crying Baby in the next room. So you may want to ask another Mother (neighbor) to supervise while you run to the short erand. Never leave without making sure that you left Baby's Milk and/ or a pacifier in case the child awakens.

Of course, a newborn child will always attract attention, no matter where you take the child. Please, Monitor who you allow to hold your child. Every person has good intentions, but not everyone knows how to properly hold a newborn child. The childs Head and Neck must always be supported properly. So you may have to demonstrate to the person how you would like to have your child held. Remember, this your child and how he is handled is very important. "SO WHAT!!!!!" You may embarrass someone by showing how to hold your child "SO WHAT!!!!" I don't care who the person is . . . . family or foe. You make sure that your child is safe.

(2) *TIPS FOR THE NEWBORN*

Please do not fall into that old family trick of allowing another small child to hold your newborn for any reason. I know that it will make a cute picture for the family photo album, but you take responsibility and handle your newborn. If you take care of your child today, there will be another occassion at age two that you may take another cute picture. Tell drunk Aunt Julie, *not today*!!! Maybe next time, your child is very sleepy, so just look at her . . . . for now, thank you!!!

Be aware of people kissing your child or putting their hands in your child's face. A newborn has not the immunal system to resist many BACTERIA which people carry on their hands or also their mouths. It seems that everyone wants to put their dirty, nasty hands on a baby's face (his cheeks) Please have the courage to pull away with your baby, when people try to put their hands on your child's face. Keep Baby Wipes handy, to immediately wipe away those Mascara laced kisses to your child's face. Be aware that your child could be allergic to some of those Lipstick products (Makeup). Also, watch for other small children putting their dirty little hands onto your child while he or she is laying in the crib or stroller. Your newborn will have enough coughs and sneezes, they do not need unnecessary Bacterial rashs from someone's dirty hands in his face.

Please counsel with your Doctor or a Pediatrician about Beast Feeding or other Dietary questions. What was good for your neighbor's child, may not be good for your child. Despite the fact, that you as a parent do not see your Doctor on a regular basis, Please have your child seen by a Doctor on a regular basis. If you do not feel confident in your family Doctor for whatever reason. Look in the Telephone Book for a Childrens Hospital or a Childrens Clinic in your city, and Please go there. Their Specialty is Children just like yours. Your child's nutrition is very important to healthy growth. So, please, seek advice to provide a healthy diet for your child. If your find yourself in a situation, that you cannot afford food for you or your child. There are Government programs that provided financial help for food and shelter. You would look in the telephone book in the Government pages under "*DSHS*" or Public Health Services. There are programs such as "*WIC*" (women, infants, children).

(3)   *NEWBORNS*

These programs were set up to help young families who are struggling financially. There is no shame to struggle financially. Hard times can happen to anyone, but it is a shame to not use resources that are available to you and your family when you need it. It does not matter if you are struggling because of some kind an addiction. No matter if Drugs or alcohol or whatever, your children don't have to suffer, there is help available to you. Please, please do not allow Pride or Shame to prevent you to seek assistance for your children. Please understand, it is not a crime to not have the money to provide food and housing for your children, but it is a crime if you do nothing and Neglect the care and well being of your children. Yes, Child Neglect is a Criminal Offense. If you are a young Mother with a newborn and you feel overwhelmed with the child. Please look up the *"DSHS"* office in your city and go there. They have a Child protection Service that will find appropriate shelter for your child. This service is also extended to Mothers and children who are living in a very violatile situation. Even if you know of someone who is living with a small child in a very dangerous environment. Please, be their friend, help them to get to one of these agencies for help. I guarantee that they will thank you later.

Another very important fact to remember, your Newborn child should always be strapped into a child safety seat while traveling in a motor vehicle. This is very important because should your vehicle have to make a sudden stop. Your Newborn does not have the developed muscles to brace himself to prevent bodily damage. Please use the proper seat size for your child. These seats provide the proper support for your child when needed. I know that most young parents feel that they can hold the child while riding in a car. But most accidents happen suddenly, that adult parent's body weigh might harm the child as much as the collision itself. In a car accident, it is tough enough for an adult to control his reactive movement, It is twice as hard to protect a child safely. So, please make certain that your child has the proper car seating. If not, then maybe your child should not be riding on this trip. Ask yourself, how important is your child's safety to you and your family. *DON'T TAKE THE CHANCE*!!!! At least, your child will be alive to take another car ride properly seated. You, as the Parent, need to *BUCKLE UP*!!!! also because that child needs you alive.

(4) *NEWBORNS*

On the Market today, you will find many different types of transportation devices for your child. Devices such; Baby Back harnesses and Baby strollers. In your household you can find many items that you can bargain basement shop for certain items. But when it comes to the safety of your child, do not look to save money by buying the cheapest one. For example: Some Baby Back Harnesses do not give proper support for the height and weight of your child. Be very careful in the Purchase of this type of item. It could cause a permanent bodily injury to your child. So, pay the money for a safe one. The same goes for a strollers. You may need to ask the Store Manager which strollers are returned the most because of mechanical defects, and do not buy that one regardless of the store discount. You do not want your child's stroller to break down and cause harm to your child. Prevent a problem down the road (later), so buy a good one. Buy a stroller that he can grow (room to grow) into safely.

There will be those family members who will want to buy clothing for the child or give to you clothing (hand-me-downs) that their children once wore. Be careful, make sure that the clothing fits your child. For example, Shoes, which are very difficult to fit. Some children have wide feet, some have very narrow feet. Broad shoulders or wide neck sizes. Loose fitting clothing are the very best. Children outgrow their clothing over night. Do not put Girl clothing on a little Boy, because these are the formattive years of a child's life. By cross dressing a small child may subject that child to unnecassary ridicule (teasing) by other small children. Believe or not, children can be very cruel to one another, when teasing playfully. So even at an early age, do not subject your child to unnecessary teasing. For example: do not put ribbons in a boy's hair, or pegtails. This may be cool to you as an alternative lifestyle adult, but give your child a chance at having some normalcy in his life. Do not put him or her in a position to be labeled as "Weird" so early in their life. Do not set them up to be "Scared" phycologically, they will have plenty of time to make lifestyle statements as teenagers, you just wait.

CHAPTER VIII

TURNING

    TERRIBLE

        TWO'S

INTO

    TREMENDOUS

        THREE'S

TURNING THE TERRIBLE TWO'S INTO TREMENDOUS THREES

Fear of the Unknown is one habitual trait that all humans embrace very quickly. Once the Fear Factor been removed and replaced by the mere knowledge that "THING" . . . . that we feared is achievable or conquerable. The parameters or borders are immediately increased. Wisdom and Knowledge are two mighty vehicles (Tools) which will always resolve any dilemma. Now the proper use of Wisdom and knowledge will deliver Understanding. Many Educators have said "In all your getting, strive to get an Understanding", of your children, as well as other family members. As a Parent, you are always seeking A *BETTER WAY* (Wisdom & Knowledge). However, understanding "WHY" your child behaves the way that they do, will greatly affect your Parenting Techniques. For example: If you are approached by an Intoxicated (Drunken) Person, who is making non-sensical remarks about you. Despite the fact, this Drunk person is saying very rude words. Through your Wisdom and Knowledge, you have assessed that this person is Drunk and has lost his rational judgement. In other words, he is not making any sense, plus he is staggering in his walk, along with very slerded speech. You know how to properly react (or respond) to that person.

Now, that same example applies to your child, whom you will need to begin to observe and Understand his or her Inquirering Mind. Which seems to function in overdrive all the time. Please discard all of the stories that you have heard about the *TERRIBLE TWOs*' (Two Year olds). You can turn your child into a *TERRIFIC TWO* or even a *TREMENDOUS THREE*. You must exercise every ounce of understanding towards your Two or Three year old child.

****Again, always remember, "NOTHING IS MORE IMPORTANT THAN THE WAY THAT YOU REACT TOWARDS IT."****

At the ages of 2 and 3, All children . . . . that's right!!! I said it, "ALL CHILDREN!" are very inquisitive at this age. They are always exploring, prying, peeping, snooping, touching, tasting, or just plain meddling where they should NOT be. This is a Natural Behavior at this age. Your child is not acting this way to upset you nor trying to get on your last nerve. This is just a phase that will past away.

This is the stage of you child's life which curiousity will get the better of him or her. Your child is not acting out of disobedience towards you nor trying to draw negative attention. Your child is playfully exploring Life's boundaries and parameters.

I am always amazed at the patience and restraints of most Pet owners when they return home to find their living quarters in a shamble, as the result of leaving their lovable little Dog or Cat home alone. So, why does our society view young innocent, yet immature children so differently?? Why should a child know better (when left alone)?? Why should they be less playful??? Why should they not think that Mommy's Hair Dryer is not a Cool Looking Space Gun???? Or that Daddy's Ties make great rope for tying up Imaginary Bad Guys???

In your child's Mind (Eye): Why waste Mommy's expensive Bathe Oil on Mommy alone . . . . Let's pour enough Bathe Oil in our bath water to make "SUPER BUBBLES", enough bubbles for all his imaginary friends that we Adults cannot see physically????

Your child views the World around him very innocently, playfully, without a care in the World. They will not function responsibly. When they spill the box of Cereal on the floor, they believe that another box of Cereal will automatically grow back in the cabinet. Better yet, when they spill the Juice all over the table, they think that Mommy has a Juice Cow hiding somewhere . . . waiting to fill the empty carton with more Juice, for later when they get thirsty again.

A CHILD'S FAVORITE WORD BECOMES "WHY" !!!!!

This period of your child's life can be referred to as the beginning of the "WHY" period. You, as a parent, will understand when every response to whatever you say is "WHY". It will really challenge your patience when every response will be "WHY".

EXAMPLE: Go to your room!! Why?? Now!!! Why?? Brush your teeth!! Why?? Don't pet the dirty dog!!! Why?? Because I said so!!! Why?? Eat your vegetables!! Why?? Because vegetables are good for you!!! Why?? Just eat your food!!! Why??

Now, this is not the time to start changing your haircolor. But it is time that you can begin to teach your child . . . all those good and wonderful values that we all have been waiting to teach. With lots of love and patience, We begin this teaching process fully understanding why our child is acting this way and responding to us the way that they do. Let us always try to approach our Lovable little Darlings with understanding and positive compassion. They are really not trying to get on your last nerve.

Now, scientifically speaking, you can begin teaching values and boundaries at age nine months. We may think that we are wasting our time and energy, talking to our infants. But even at nine months of age, they begin to understand and comprehend your instructions. Please remember, when you are teaching children, consistent repetition is critical. You will feel like a broken record when you find yourself repeating do's and don'ts to your child. Keep in mind that the only boundaries that your child knows are the ones that you have taught them. If you did not tell them not to do something, please do do not expect your child to know on their own. You may show by example, not telling them only.

You must be very, very specific in our instructions at this age. For example: "*Darling, take your toys to your room?*" Okay first, "bend over and pick-up your toys in your hands". "Now, hold the toys tightly in your hands." "Now walk down the hall and go into your room". "Now, walk over to your toybox, take the top off your toybox, and place your toys into your toybox." "Please put the top back onto your toybox and walk back here to Mommy." This is an example, at first, please make your instructions super simple and easy to understand for them to learn.

CHAPTER IX

B   E

CONSISTENT:

****

"SAY WHAT YOU MEAN,

MEAN WHAT YOU SAY"

BE CONSISTENT

To flourish, children need not only "loving" but "consistency" in their homes. Be consistent in the way you discipline and punish your children for misbehaving. It is normal for children to test the limits of their parents and other adults. If as a parent you are inconsistent, then you are in a sense encouraging more misbehavior from your children.

Be consistent in your rules, so that your child will learn from early age the predictable consequences for any of his misbehaviors. For example, if one of your household rules includes not jumping on the sofa, if you catch your child, be consistent and reprimand him accordingly. Do not ignore the misdeed, and, therefore, convey the message that he or she can get away with it now and maybe even later. Although remember not be extra strict, either, such as by grounding your child for a month. Make sure your child understands that it is his misbehavior that upsets you and that you will always love him.

Through these home rules you are teaching your children respect. Do not ignore rude behavior at home, for you cannot excuse your children's misbehavior in public. The good behavior that originates from home is what grandparents refer to as "home training." When an elderly person responds with "does that child have any home training?" the reference is to a child's discipline at home.

In a consistent disciplining environment, it is important to make sure that the rules are enforced by both parents. Therefore, parents should be in agreement when it comes to disciplining their child. Truthfully, it is easier said than done, for in today's society we have more broken homes than we have had say twenty years ago. With staggering divorce and marriage failure statistics, broken homes are becoming more and more acceptable as normal.

By a broken home, I refer to a household in which a father and a mother figure of a child live separated. Whether due to a divorce or separation, the father or the mother no longer enjoys open communications with the child. The parent in custody has daily contact with the child, therefore, is responsible for establishing most of child's rules in and out of home. The problem may arise when that child will visit the second parent during the weekends.

During the visitations, it would be natural for the second parent to fall into a trap of actually, although not maliciously, spoiling the child. The reasoning behind it: it is only for a weekend, what can it hurt. In some cases, the parental guidance might even turn into parental rivalry, competing for the child's love and affection, by always trying to be the favorite parent to the child. The rules of the main household, therefore, might not even be enforced on weekends, causing problematic loss of discipline consistency in child's life. Two parents might have different set of rules for the same child to follow, forcing the child to take on multiple acceptable behaviors. These parents will lose their focus of raising a well-balanced child.

It is very difficult to establish consistency in a broken home. If there is a slightest of possibilities in keeping the family together through religious (clergy) or professional counseling, in most cases, it will benefit the children. In today's society, it really takes two parents, working together to provide the attention necessary to raise well-balanced, successful children.

II)   SAY WHAT YOU MEAN, MEAN WHAT YOU SAY

Saying what you mean has a follow-up of honesty and the keeping of your word. If you say to you child that you are going to do something, by all means follow thru. The worst thing that you can do to your children is to build a track record of dishonesty.

You see, children cannot distinguish between when you are telling the truth or just spouting out (shallow nonsense) threats. The worst image that your child could have of you, is that your words are meaningless and not be taken seriously (or beleived). We make jokes about the children folktale of "the boy who cried wolf". For those of you who are not familiar with the story: A little boy always made jokes about a hungry wolf being in the area, so he cried "WOLF, WOLF". After several weeks, no one listened to the little boy, nor believed him. One day a real wolf appeared and the little boy was eaten by the wolf because no one heeded his cries.

So, please follow thru with action to whatever you say. And by all means, KEEP YOUR WORD AND PROMISES TO YOUR CHILDREN!!!!!!!

CHAPTER X

ARE

YOU

A

CONSIDERATE

PARENT

****

CONTROL

YOUR:

VOICE, ACTIONS, REACTIONS

ARE YOU A CONSIDERATE PARENT???

Children are a handful of responsibility. You know that you have to keep an eye and an ear on them constantly, especially on the newborns and the toddlers. Toddlers have a talent of creating a mess within a matter of minutes. Whether in private or public, you as a parent should always be in control of your small children.

What does it mean to be a considerate parent? Let me give you an illustration of pet owners who love and treat their pets like children. Many of them will ignore the "wrongs" of their pets toward strangers by seeing those acts as "cute." People walking their dogs allow their pets to rub up against strangers or slobber saliva on their clothing. The usual response from the pet owner would be, "oh, come here, Fluffy . . . don't bother that nice man." I am sure that the reason that the nice man was walking through the area was not in search for a reason to polish his shoes or dry clean his slacks once more. A different illustration with cats—allowing them to climb on the laps of the strangers without a second thought that the person might be allergic. These illustrations display little consideration for others.

The same can be said about little children. People might not be allergic to little kids, but not everyone has the same depth of love and high toleration towards them. It is fair for people to expect you as parents to keep your children disciplined and under control at all times.

Your child's public behavior reflects his private discipline. Prior to leaving your home take a toy with you that would occupy your child's attention the longest. In addition, bring with you an activity that you might do together, such as read a book or play with a story puppet. Such would especially be needed during traveling, i.e. taking your child on an airplane, bus, or train. Passengers around do have the right to a peaceful, relaxing flight, minus yells of young children. If you must use public transportation in your travels, check with your pediatrician for a mild child's sedative to allow your child to fall asleep. At a very early age, do not put your infant through long trips. Rather, consider having the grandparents visit your family instead. If that is not possible, then use private transportation, such as a rental car or a private plane. If you search the internet or some newspapers, you may be surprised to find out how many different forms of private transportation may be available in your area.

In your home, always have a list of local babysitters available, preferably mature teenagers who have taken a babysitting course offered in community and adult education centers. Use the list if you are planning to attend a special event or hear a guest speaker. If you cannot find an available babysitter, consider staying at home with your child instead. If you do decide on taking your child with you, in case of misbehavior, be courteous and dismiss yourself and your child. Standing by the open doors of the auditorium and attempting to calm the screams of your child while catching only half of the speech is not a wise option. As lovely as the voice of your child might be, few listeners would want it as the background noise on their recordings of the speech.

CONTROL YOUR TONE OF VOICE, ACTIONS, REACTIONS

As a parent, you will develop emotional self-control—ability to control your actions and reactions. "Actions" mean your outward display of feelings toward certain events. For example: the manner in which you will give instructions to your child going out the door while on the phone with your not-so-very-pleasant mother-in-law. Would your words to your child reflect unearned irritation, or would you be speaking to him calmly?

"Reactions" are your responses toward another's actions. When a child is hit by his playmate, the child's natural reaction is to punch back. Now as adults, we are expected to respond more maturely. The question is whether your response would be a positive one or negative. A positive response would be: "Johnny, that was not a nice thing to do . . . I am really surprised that you punched. Johnny is a nice boy, and nice boys do not punch people. I know that you did not purposefully do that . . . did you? I know you didn't . . . . Johnny, you are a nice boy and I love you." In contrast to a positive response a parent might respond with a slap back against the child's back followed by the yelling: "You little brat!! I should knock you out for doing that!! Now shut the #$%^ up!! You should not have punched me, you little #$%@# brat!!!"

Here we had two contrasting responses, portraying control of one's reaction. Remember the golden rule that there is nothing more important to your child's development than the way you react to a situation. When your child misbehaves, stop! Take a deep breath to give yourself a chance to push aside your true feelings of frustration and anger. Think. Think clearly about your next step! Speak in a calm tone of voice (even if you do not feel calm at the moment) and pronounce positive words of hope, words projecting to your child your faith in his goodness, even if his present actions might not reflect it. Controlled positive reaction would require many rehearsals until it will become easier and easier to perform.

In previous chapters, we learned that children are like little mirrors, or sponges that soak in their surrounding environment. Parents are children's first and longest books that children will ever read, so why not be a best example in your child's life. What type of self-image would you want your child to have as he grows up: a good, likable individual or a never-do-good, disappointment of a person? If a child hears negative responses often enough, he will eventually embrace and act on them.

Please do not perceive this chapter as a harsh criticism, but rather as a given opportunity for change. A first-born does not come with a manual, so please do not feel condemned by any ideas discussed within this chapter. Regardless of past experiences with your child, you do have the ability to change as a parent. Perhaps not overnight, but a step at a time—altering your mindset towards children. Moreover, who knows, maybe you are a motherly person to whom children would be naturally drawn. In the after-school hours, you might find your house full of children's laughter, and not just those of your own. You might become a talk of the PTA meetings—not negative gossip but rather admiring comments. You might be complimented on how well behaved your children are in the classroom (such a rare occurrence at our day and age) and how good-natured your attitude has become! All these bonuses are the results of you willing to become a better parent.

Reject an old negative saying that children will drive you crazy; rather, embrace Biblical truth that children are little blessings from God.

CHAPTER XI

DISCIPLINE

THE

CHILD

WHEN

YOUNG

DISCIPLINE A CHILD WHEN YOUNG

Within the following pages, I will be sharing what I have found to be effective in my experience of raising four successful, mentally stable children. There is an old cliché that I have found to be true, "spare the rod, and spoil the child." It is not a mere oldwife's tale, but rather a Biblical principal from the book of Proverbs, known to be as one of the books of wisdom. While researching this proverb, I have stumbled upon a similar verse: if a parent does not discipline a child, the child will bring his parents to an open shame (paraphrased). A simple illustration would be witnessing an embarrassing public display i.e. an exhausted mother trying to handle an out-of-control toddler in the middle of a store aisle. In the throes of one's temper tantrum the child is oblivious to his mother's threats.

Within my household, my wife and I outlawed any form of a temper tantrum. A temper tantrum or a physical fight with one's sibling would result in the suspension of all fun privileges as well as in a spanking on the buttocks with the infamous giant, plastic spoon. We never allowed ourselves to discipline our own children with a bare hand. Nor did we continue if we were upset and unable to direct our full attention to disciplining. Within our household all spanking or paddling was performed with two particular items: 1) a large plastic (rubber-like) flat stirring spoon, or 2) a smooth, lightweight wooden spoon. These spoons were just large enough to fit within my wife's shoulder bag. Additionally, I was able to carry one of them in my back pants pocket. After a few spanking sessions, we discovered that merely showing our child the spoon of correction with an option of earning a spanking at home was enough of an incentive for a better behavior.

In the act of spanking, there are general Do's and Don'ts. I have little toleration for child abuse and brutality. Spanking is an act that parents should never enjoy performing. Because of my love toward my children, I hated to have to spank them, causing them physical pain. When I chose to spank them, I always performed it with the spoon of correction against the "meatiest" part of their bodies—the buttocks, knowing that it will not cause them permanent damage. Be careful not to spank near child's genital area. Never use any objects, such as belts, cords, sticks, hairbrushes, kitchen/garden utensils that might pierce, cut or damage child's body in any away. The child should clearly understand why he or she is being punished. Allowing him or her to ask questions is essential to child's development.

Prior to embarking on the act of spanking, place yourself in your child's shoes. Do not rush to punish the child, but rather stop and think through the child's behavior. Think about the circumstances that might have influenced your child's actions. Do not ever voice such phrases, as "You are no good! You are always bad! You will never amount to anything!!!" Too many upset parents will react negatively to a smallest mishap. The parent must stop himself before reacting irrationally. Nothing is more important than the way the parent reacts to the incident. In such cases, the parent needs to calm down, gather senses and composure before taking any further action. Parents have the power to crush their child's feelings with harsh words. A child always seeks an approval from his parents. So when a parent reacts by screaming, the child will be scarred emotionally.

If the child earned a time out, do not pounce upon the child as soon as he is done. Many a times the child might be fuming over his "unfair" punishment. If that is the case, let the child express his feelings, for you do not want him to remain angry with you. Communicate to the child your love for them by coming to some agreement and pleasant understanding. In addition, suggest an activity that both you and a child can do together. Children are different in areas of forgiving and forgetting. A child releases a problem much sooner. Holding grudges is a lesson our children learn from observing adults.

If you as a parent have grown up in an abusive household, I strongly urge you to seek therapy as soon as possible. As a parent, you should be psychologically balanced prior to embarking any physical disciplining upon your own child. A rule of thumb to remember: never discipline your child when angry, upset, or mentally unbalanced. During the disciplining, you need to be fully conscious and aware of your disciplinary actions. You need to be acting out of love, rather than be provoked into it. Once again, I urge you to seek professional counseling to develop legitimate family disciplinary policies, especially if this is your first child. Disciplining your child is never fun, but is essential. Proper discipline at an early age will save much trouble later.

In summary, allow me to make a few points more clearer. When disciplining your child, please make the punishment fit the crime. In other words, do not over-react to every little incident with your child. A child's heart is filled with playful folly and fun. Your child does not consider consequences during their every day activities. So, do not hesitate to talk with other Parents about certain activities of your child. Something that you may feel is a big problem, may just be a minor activity to others. You do not want to fall into the trap of feeling your child's activities are so enormous when in reality they are not. In other words, do not make a mountain out of a little mold hill. Remember, every little incident does not need harsh or even mild discipline. Many problems can be solved with just a good "Talking To" about it. Your child may not realize that a certain activity really upsets you. Better communication may be your solution in some cases.

Also, each child has a different temperment. Some children require much less disciplinary actions than other children. I remember in my own experiences, one of my children was so sensitive. That if I were to raise my voice towards my youngest child in any way, it was the same as if she had been spanked. You, as a parent, must understand the differences with regards to disciplining your children. Please recognize the different in a strong-willed child and a mischievous child. I can almost guarantee you that the mischievous child has learned that behavior from another child or a rude adult, that the child has been exposed to little too much. For the strong-willed child, do not feel that you must break that strong-will. But rather, you need to find ways to channel that strong energy into positivity. You may not believe it, but that strong willness may guide that child into tremendous Goal-Setting and a high level of drive towards accomplishment and achievement. There are books written by experts, on channeling the energy of the strong-willed child. Again, treat each of your children as an individual according to his or her temperment. Discipline in Love first, that will always pay-off in the Long run of life.

CHAPTER XII

ALLOW

YOUR

CHILD

SPACE

TO

GROW

ALLOW YOUR CHILD SPACE TO GROW

Regardless of age, every individual needs room to grow. In other words, we all need space and opportunity to succeed, or even fail in some occasions. As loving, caring parents, we never wish to see our child in need, lack, or hurt—so we have this tendency to control and even maybe smother our children's growth. The reality is that with increasing age there is only so much of our child's world that we as parents can control. It is a difficult discipline to be a simple spectator in our child's world, but we must take that step to allow our children the chance to find his or her own niche in this world. On their own! Even in nature, as we observe animals and insects, we notice that the newborns must use their own strength and abilities to come out of their shells, literally speaking. Their parents are present to guide, teach, train, but mainly to set the example.

Children of all ages learn best in a safe environment within their homes. At an infant stage, allow your child to grow by having plenty of safe space for rolling and crawling in order to encourage natural exploration. Babies are curious about any and every object, so please make sure to have enough baby toys available at hand. It is also, therefore, important to remember to child-proof all places where you will be spending time with your child. Encourage your baby to craw by placing a toy almost within his reach, and watch the progress from sidelines. Be there for your baby in case of any mishaps, but do give your baby a chance to get the toy himself.

Babies need opportunities to develop their upper body strength and such can be done by rolling and throwing balls, and at later stages, by crawling and pulling themselves up. Take that extra time to play games with your baby in order to gently encourage him to use his arms and legs to work his muscles. Although do make sure that the clothing you put on your child are loose enough not to hinder his arm and leg movement in the play. Any kind of play will allow children to try out and practice their new skills.

As your child reaches toddler stage, he might be more skilled at feeding himself, but as a parent you will have your hands full trying to satisfy his other hunger—hunger for new experiences. As they are starting to walk, the children will need opportunities to strengthen their lower bodies by walking and jumping. Encourage your child to do variety of physical activities to help his coordination and movement such as running or walking up and down the stairs, but make sure not to pressure him into something he might not be yet comfortable with. Remember that all children are different, and all need time and space to grow.

Later in life, the child will start using colored pencils and doing puzzles, which will greatly help his eye-hand coordination. These activities at first might be new and very tiring to your children, so do not expect them spend a lot of time on these. The first drawn letters or numbers might be barely recognizable, but do continue practicing with them at their own speed. Any hands-on activities will help your child develop all his senses, which are sight, hearing, smell, touch, and taste. Talk to them about their senses by comparing the way different objects in their environment look, sound, feel, or even smell. This round ball is smooth and hard, while that stuffed kitty is soft and furry. Consider having your child by your side as you are preparing meals, although do keep in mind the child-proofing tips while you are in the kitchen. Allow your child to taste different kinds of foods as you are cooking in order for your child to get used to a variety of smells and tastes and maybe even different textures.

TEENAGE YEARS?

As your child grows, be sure to recognize the line between taking safety precautions and being overprotective of your child. Keep a safe environment in order to allow your child to experiment with different areas of his world. To help with the physical growth, you as parent can make sure that your child gets enough rest to function and learn during the day, nutritious food for good health, and regular exercises for developing muscles. Be an example and a guide to your child, and do have realistic expectations.

CHAPTER XIII

WHAT

WILL

BECOME

NORMAL

BEHAVIOR

TO

YOUR

CHILD

WHAT WILL BECOME NORMAL BEHAVIOR IN YOUR CHILD'S MIND

Younger children are like sponges. They are continually absorbing (thru their senses) the sights and sounds around their world. The old notion of: "Do as I say, not as I do because I am a grown-up". Has and will never work with children!!! Why?? Because the computer brain of children is contually collecting data on things that a child sees and hears around him. While, we as parents try to talk and communicate with the Conscious part of the Child's Brain, the Subconscious part of the Brain is continually collecting data.

An example of this: A parent can talk or verbalize to their child that drinking alcohol is bad for them. The Child's subconscious part of his Brain sees (1) Uncle Joe or possibly his Dad in a drunken condition periodically, (2) every time the *child* opens the refrigerator, he sees a six-pack of beer. Over the years, the child's Brain reconfirms that these two points are normal in his household: (1) That periodically it is perfectly normal for the role-model head of household to be found in a drunken condition, and (2) it is completely normal for the refrigerator to have at least one six-pack of beer in it. It is abnormal if there is no beer in the refrigerator. Now, let us take that one step further. What if the child's Brain sees the drunken role-model male (his Father or the mom's boyfriend) punching, hitting, or physically abusing his Mother. That child's conscious mind will make him cry, scream-out, say that he does not like to see these bad things done to his Mother, the woman he loves. But . . . that child's Subconscious Mind is recording all these actions as normal behavior in his household when his male role-model Drinks. So guess what!!!! When that child grows into adulthood, He will probably speak out the feelings of his conscious mind, that he hated his Father's abusive actions . . . hurting his Mother, but, deeply tucked away in his Subconscious regions of his mind. His brain has recorded that hitting the woman that you love when drunken is a normal behavior. As a result . . . . you guessed it!!! When the Son (now an adult) is in a drunken condition/ or high on drugs, his consciuos mind is now blurred . . . his Subconscious mind mind takes over and starts in with recorded normal behaviors for this frame of mind . . . . which is imitate the actions of that male role-model . . . on the woman that he loves. This momentary Subconscious mind take over is experienced by many people when they are driving home from their every day job, the Driver of the car has so many things on his or her mind of chores that they wish to accomplish when they arrive home. Their subconscious mind drives the car home while their conscious mind organizes their chores. Upon arrival at their home the driver the car cannot recall any of the events while driving home. The driver feels some what of a time lapse in the time their subconscious mind began driving the car home, and the conscious events along the way. The common response is: Wow!! How did I get home so fast!!!

Let's take another example: THE way that you speak to your small child can and will affect your child's self-esteem (THE WAY that he or she views himself). Let us say that your young child accidentally breaks a very valuable piece of furniture. Now Parents please remember this very Important quote: "THERE IS NOTHING MORE IMPORTANT IN LIFE THAN THE WAY THAT WAY THAT YOU REACT TO IT" Now this ouote can be applied to any situation. For example: Your infant is starting to walk and she falls down. At first, the child does not know how to respond to her falling. If the child's parent comes running and screaming out," OH my baby!!! Are you hurt!! The child will most likely begin to cry as a response to the mother's actions. On the other hand, if the mother approached the fallen child smiling, almost laughing, speaking in a soft tone of voice saying, "My funny little Girl . . . . you are doing good . . . walking for mommy, my baby, my good baby"!!! I bet that the fallen child will react to your smiling and will not cry.

Let us get back to your young child who just broke a valuable piece of furniture. You as the Parent must stop and think quickly, "WHICH IS MORE IMPORTANT TO YOU???? YOUR CHILD OR THE BROKEN FURNITURE???? Hopefully your child . . . . Now, treat the situation accordingly.

Never call your child Inferior Names: "You No Good Jerk!!! you clumsy little x@#$¢%&!!!! Instead, Take a deep breathe/ or a time out moment. Then respond: "I'm really surprised at you . . . . This is not like you because you are a good son, you are not a clumsy boy, you do not play with Mommy and daddy's valuable furniture. I am very sad and surprised at what you have done. But Mommy Loves you because you will not do this kind of thing to mommy and daddy's things again???? Will you???

CHAPTER XIV

FAMILY

TIME

FAMILY TIME

A great communication tool to implement a more open form of communication for all family members. *FAMILY TIME* is a predesignated time each week, where the entire family can assemble for the purpose of communication *only!* This *FAMILY TIME* is free of all outside distractions. For example: *NO T.V., Radios,* all the *Telephones* are *tuned OFF, No* Guests allowed . . . . just the immediate family! This family time must be consistant each week! This is an event that should never be cancelled or postponed. It should only be shortened, in case of a family conflict. This event should be scheduled around by the entire family, as a *Major Event!* Family Time should be established as soon as the youngest Family member can talk. This Family moment should consist of a minimum of one hour. An hour of open communications As your children become older this will rapidly become one of the fastest hours of the week, simply because of the increased conversations.

The *GROUND RULES* for *FAMILY TIME:*

(1) Every Family member may speak honestly and freely
(2) *No* Punishment will be enforced for anything revealed during the Family Time Period, (in other words, No child can be punished for any wrong deeds exposed).

******* During these sessions you will find out just how that Lamp was broken*******

(3) *NO COMMENT* will be viewed as stupid or not important. (in other words, something that may seem silly from a small child, may be very important to the feelings of that child!)
(4) *NO!!!* Laughing at someone's statement!! Again, during this time period, *NO* subject is considered Taboo, Nor Sacred!! (in other words, any subject may be discussed).

This *FAMILY TIME* will be most effective when the Parents and children view this as a *discussion period* and *NOT!!! NOT!!!* a *LECTURE Time* by the Parents!!! Parents will learn about their children's world, when they sit back and listen to the opinions of their children's point of view. The Parents should also open up and reveal some of their childhood experiences into the discussion. As time goes on, these sessions should make everyone feel comfortable in discussing their true feelings and problems. These Family Time Sessions will help to bridge the generation communication gaps and keep Parents in touch with the peer pressures, changes, and other development in their children's lives.

For example: At the start of the Family time sessions your Six year old Daughter may want to talk about Little billy, Who pushes her down on the playground during Recess at school. When she is seventeen, she will want to discuss something said to her by timothy, who is a senior from another school.

My own personal experience as a Father of four. My children are now ages 29, 27, 26, 23, they all have their own lives and living in different cities. However, we still meet together at least once every two months at a pre-chosen Restaurant. There we resume our Adult to Adult version of our *Family Time*. As usual, we discuss any new changes in our lives, then we procede with our Round-Table Problem Solving session for any individual challenges anyone is facing.

Beleive me the earlier you start to implement this open forum of communication the better. The later that you wait to start communicating it will be harder to open up to one another's feelings.

******* Parents it is very important that you open up to your children in these discussions. At first, when your children are very young, please respect their young ages. *Do not* lay a lot of heavy stuff on your kids, like Ex: Mother and Daddy were fighting this week . . . NO!! NO!! NO!! *TOO MUCH* for younger children. Instead Say: "Your Mommy and Daddy had a very difficult week, so we are very sorry that if we may have raised our voices aroud the house. But always remember that your Mommy and Daddy love each other just as we will always Love you Children. Sorry kids, but when your Daddy is tired of something . . . . Daddy will accidentally raise his voice. But please do not worry . . . . Everything will be alright." This is a little softer for a child.***********

Now, as your children become older in age. You can begin to share a little more of your daily challenges at the office and with other people. Allow your family to get to know you as a Father and a person. Do not expect your children to open up and reveal their true feelings . . . . while you as a Parent continue to hide your feelings. Please keep a discussion session and not shouting match between siblings. Always promote Family Unity in these sessions, and working together to resolve issues.

******* Remember, these sessions goal is to open communications and bring the Family closer together in Love. End each session by having everyone to said the words "I Love You" to other Family members. Parents, you must take the lead in this . . . . You start by saying, "I Love You" to each family member. After several months, it will become a habit.***********

By understanding the main concept of this book, that children are little mirrors of whom???? Us??? Our surroundings??? Our Parents??? Our views and our opinions???? Our bias and prejudices??? Our association

The Images that we create for our children are very influential. Today, Most people have very busy schedules, leaving *NO* time for the children that we brought into this world which should be our priority. A very important truth that I will share with you . . . please remember it: THE MORE TIME THAT BOTH PARENTS SPEND WITH THEIR CHILD OR CHILDREN . . . . THE LESS TIME THAT YOU WILL SPEND WHEN THEY ARE TEENAGERS . . . GETTING THEM OUT OF TROUBLE." Today's parents are very career oriented. In other Words, their individual careers come first. When the company says, "you (one of the Parents) must fly out to Japan on Business for three weeks. That Parent Jumps and says this Business trip to Japan is of higher priority than my being with my family. Possibly missing several important evewnts in your child's Life. These are very special moments that you will never be able to re-live with your child again. That Parent will always use the excuse that, "I AM DOING THIS FOR THE FAMILY . . . TO BETTER PROVIDE FOR MY FAMILY."

"T I M E" is the one element that makes all people equal. Every human being is given 24 hours each day. How we spend those 24 hours separates us from all other creatures on the Earth . . . . It is totally up to us. "Time really Flys" in respect to our children growing up. Just ask any GrandParent. Unfortunately, when we use up our time . . . . we will never get another opportunity at reliving that time differently. Our children support and security during their growing years. One of the ways that Support and Security is expressed . . . is in the Parent's involvement in their child's Life. Children really appreciate it when the Parents really make that effort to be there at the child's Christmas play, Soccer game, or Little league game. When your child looks out into the audience to share the moment, and sees their

Parent smiling back proudly at them. As a parent you will never find out the importance of those moments of support really meant to your child until they become Teenagers.

Teenagers have a very special gift of memory, very a often making reference to those events that you were / or were not there for them.

Always remember, "the most important thing that you can give to your child *IS YOUR TIME*."

A formula that will work for *MOST* children:

> "The Amount of Quality Time that you spend with your Child (will minus)
>
> "The Amount of Time you will spend in the Future Getting Your Child Out of Trouble"

Spending Quality Time is time you spend Interacting or Communicating with your child. Just being available and accessible in the home to listen and interact with you children is also helpful.

CHAPTER XV

YOUR-IN-LAWS

YOUR-OUT-LAWS

AND

OTHER

INFLUENCES

YOUR IN-LAWS, YOUR OUT-LAWS
& OUTSIDE INFLUENCES

It is known that the second leading cause of divorce today happens to be outside influence. In most family settings, this subject, the example of which includes grandparents spoiling their grandchildren, is generally accepted as trivial and addressed lightly. However, this is a very serious problem which has split too many families apart, leaving a lot of children without wholesome homes.

Children need consistent set of rules in order to build a safe, stable environment to grow and mature. They should always be clear on their parents' rules and expectations. It is, therefore, essential for children to understand and recognize the chain of command within the family. That chain of authority should be defined to children starting at a very young age. We really do not wish our children to think that just because Uncle Benny or Aunt Susie gives permission that it will override any previously given instruction of the parents. You as a parent do not give up your parental rights and responsibilities just because you are temporarily out of the picture.

Let us reexamine this order within the family: the father and the mother are the ruling dictators of the family. The reason why I chose such a forceful word as "dictators" is because the parents should always be in control of setting the tone, or atmosphere, and the rules of the household. For example, the "educational tone" of the household is created by parents of high education level, who will perhaps find it essential to own a small library in the recreation room and dictate the type of computers and educational software is to be allowed. If either of the parent show artistic tendencies, then the house will reflect it in the different art objects within its interior decorating; these parents would perhaps want to expose their children to different arts. A musically inclined parent will make a decision on whether piano or violin lessons are expected as part of their children's upbringing. A health-conscious parent will set healthy nutrition and exercise as top priorities.

Although it is not easy to set up the stage for the grandparents to have an active role in your children's life, one must keep in mind the wonderful benefits that your children will gain from their grandchildren-grandparent relationship. Grandparents do not have the direct responsibility of raising a child; therefore, they happen to be more lax in discipline, showing their unconditional love through extra ice cream, candies, and presents. In addition, to "spoiling," your parents might be accustomed to completely different child-rearing practices; therefore, you will probably have quite a few disagreements with your parents over how to raise your child. Although you must keep in mind that as unreasonable as their arguments might sound to you, they have your child's best interests at heart; hence, it will be best to solve any disagreements peacefully.

You should talk to your parents or other in-laws about any child-rearing conflicts that may come up openly and calmly, rather than defensively and aggressively. You need to make sure that you clearly convey to them rules and morals you want your child raised with. You must calmly but firmly insist on your relatives to respect your parental decisions and to agree to act in accordance with your beliefs and values. Although as a parent you might still have to be at least a little flexible on trivial issues, such as a bit too much ice cream or pizza on the weekends with their grandparents, even if you are very health-oriented.

During the festive times of grandparents' visits, it should be remembered that no decision of either parent can ever be overruled by a grandparent, especially by an overbearing grandmother. Many times women marry a sensitive young man who happens to be or show tendencies of being a mere grown-up "momma's boy." This type of man would be afraid to standup to his strong-willed mother in case of any grandmother-mother conflicts. In these situations, the father needs professional counseling because through his inadequacies he will expose his children to negative factors, such as timidity and fear of authority. Inside of these type of households reside negatively influential mindset that the wife is inferior to the father's mother. This is a damaging foundation to any family. An immediate family should be a healthy functional unit whose members comply with good judgments established in agreement by the parents.

CHAPTER XVI

THE

SUGAR

FACTOR

THE SUGAR FACTOR

When you think about Kids and Candy, these two words are synonymous (the same as) as a Bee attraction to honey (sweet things). Kids and Candy can also be a nightmare to a Nutritionalist, Dentist, or to a parent who is trying to settle a youngster down. Sugar seems to rush thru the veins of a youngster much like . . . . Adrenaline (the chemical) ignites a burst of energy into an Athlete. Many younger children cannot control the way that sugar reacts inside their little bodies. Many children, when they have recieved an abundance of candy (sugar), become very unruly and out of control. The sugar in sweet items such as: Cakes, cookies, candies, ice creams, etc. will also become very addicting. Much like the affects of Nicotene to cigarette smokers. In both cases, their bodies will begin to develop a craving for sweets.

Here's a little side note to the affects of sugar: Several years ago, a research team discovered that a very famous Fast-Food Chain was cooking their French Fries in a sugar based cooking oil (grease). For a number of years this Fast-Food Chain would always finish number (#1) for the best French Fries in the industry. At least until these researchers released their discovery. Since then, the Franchise is now using a more healthier cooking (less sugar) oil.

For years, some Colas had a very addicting following of people who were addicted to the Coca Plant ingredients that was used in the some soft drinks. Again, Health groups and other Petitioners have had that ingredient monitored and in some cases removed.

A child, at any age, can become addicted to the Sugar content in sweets and candies. I have seen cases where the pregnant Mother consumed (ate) a lot of sweets during her pregnancy. After birth, that child seemed to crave sweeter things.

In my own personal family, my pregnant wife consumed a lot of salty items as snacks. Low and behold, my son had a craving for salty type sweets like potato chips, pretzels, and other salty typesnacks. So during your pregnency, it would be very wise to consult with the Nutritionalist that your Doctor works with. Just about every Doctor has a list of Speialist that they can refer their Patients to see. Such as:

Nutritionalist—for Diets and eating disorders
Physical Therapist—For Exercise and other physical challenges
Neurologist—For Nerve and sleep specialist—For Post-Birth symptoms
        or sleeping problems developed from the sleep patterns of a
        Newborn Baby.

Now, there is a positive side to the Sugar Factor. In children, the affects of sugar can be exhausted through physical exercise. Children ca run and rip, jump up and down, and eventually burn off the sugar in their little bodies. So parents, who use sweets as a reward system for their kids. It would be very wise to set a time limit on when your children can eat Sugar products. In other words, if your child's Bedtime is 8:30 PM, I would set a 4:30PM cut-off time for the consumption of sweets. Again, this cut-off time for sweets should be determined by the following factors:

1) The time that you want them to settle down and get to sleep. Or to mellow out due to some other function.
2) Allow the child at least two hours to run wild in the Park or play area. I found that the cool of the evening air (in some Northern regions) helps the child to settle down.
3) Your available time to supervise this hyper activity.
4) Two hours before the time they will be expected to sit quietly; like traveling in a car. NO!! sweets in the car.

Depending on the weather conditions in your city, should also determine the amount of sugar consumption. If you live in a very Hot climate 85° plus temperatures. I would monitor closely the amount of sweets containing artificial colorings or flavorings; like popsicles, lollipops, and other artificially flavored soft drinks. I will always remember my Brother having his stomach pumped in the Hospital from eating too many cold popsicles in the hot summer months. An energy drink or water would be recommended refreshment for your children when playing hard in hot weather. Yes, the energy drink is more expensive to buy, but you can be a wise parent and add water to the energy drink (just our parents would have done). Fruits would make an excellent substitute for candies. Fruits such as: apples, oranges, cantelope, watermellon, etc.

Unlike Uncle Charlie, who swears that another morning beer is the best cure for an alcoholic hangover. If your child has a fever or a cold, sweets should not be given to a child until the child is completely recovered from his or her illness. There was an old wives fable that said, "you starve a fever or cold". In other words, you give the child plenty of (preferably) warm liquids to flush the mucus germs through the childs digestive system.

Now let us stop for a moment, before you or your partner begin to play Doctor on your child. The first thing you should do is look in the local telephone book, in the yellow pages section, under Hospitals, Nurses, or physicians. You will find a number for 1-800-___NURSE; Many Hospital and Physician Groups offer this free service by phone. This service allows you to speak one-to-one with a trained certified Nurse. Now, you can describe over the phone, your child's condition. This trained Nurse will make recommendations to you to help your child. Please be truthful and honest with this Medical Person on the phone. Because this Nurse will determine (based on the Information that you give to her) Whether or not, that you need to take your child into the nearest Hospital to see a Doctor. This Nurse will also allow you to follow-up with her. This is very important to know if your child is doing better or worse. Also, when you are talking with the phone Nurse, do not forget to tell her about any allergies or medications your child has been exposed to taking. I realize that most cases require only a good hot bowl of soup and some hot Tea. But when dealing with our children, we could all use a little Professional advice. I make this suggestion to try first, because first child parents usually go running off to the Emergency Room, at the site or sound of any type of sniffle or running nose. Then, later when you get the bill for using the Emergency room, you will wish that you had spoke with a Nurse first. Some of those Emergency Room bills can be very big. It will seem like you are paying for every Doctor who stuck his head into room with your child or spoke to your child. Also it is a good idea to keep your Family Doctor's phone number handy . . . . escpecially on your speed dial numbers.

Remember, Parents, although you may have a chocolate fetish. you must guard your child's consumption of sugar and sweets. The nutritional value in fresh vegetables will always be more beneficial to the growth of your child. So, do not allow your child to eat sugar sweets within two hours of dinner time. Sugar sweets (treats) will always kill a child's appetite for good healthy food. You can allow a larger portion of sweets after Lunch time, when your child has more time to physically burn off the sugar running and playing. Now, remember, NO sugar filled snacks before Dinner time, and a smaller portion of sugar snacks after dinner. The rule in our house was strict: No yummy desert until after you finish your dinner.

Also, Parents be careful of portions of starches that you give to your children. Starches are filler foods that we serve at dinner, such as:

Rice, Potatoes . . . etc. You see, rice and potatoes, when your child digests starches, they breakdown into a form of sugar in your child's digestive system.

So Parents, the next time that you visit your Doctor's office, ask your Doctor for a nutritional booklet for Healthier meals. Listen to your Doctor's advice for your family, over anything that I might say in this book. Many Doctors suggest: heavier on the veggies and fruits . . . but lighter on the red meats and starches . . . . and very light on the sugars.

When my children were pre-schoolers, we allowed heavier sweets after lunch and superlight deserts such as: fruits, jello, gelatins after dinner. So, at bedtime, we had no fights or bribes to get our children to settle down for bed.

CHAPTER XVII

NITE

LITES

NITE LITES

Please do not make a big issue out of this chapter. A "NITE LITE" can simply be a temporary security blanket. A Nitelite is a simple solution to some temporary fear or trauma (or Fear of the Dark). I personally feel that people make too much of a big deal over Fear Factors such as Fear of the Dark. I will admit that more evil deeds are done in the dark, much more than in a well-lighted area. I also will admit that there are healthy fears that must be acknowledged. Such as: (a) The fear of walking alone down a dark alley at night. (b) walking thru unsafe neighborhoods with the reputation of high crime. (c) the Fear of certain dangerous weather conditions. (d) Fears of certain Wild Animals, etc.

As adults, we are more capable of controlling our emotions regarding certain fears. However, children are much different, they do not understand their emotions and fears. Children can be very easily amused and they can find happiness and joy in the slightest things. Children (especially the small ones) can also be traumatize by the most trivial of events, So, please, be very patient with your child. It is very important to a child that he or she feels safe especially at night. One of the first signs of insecurity in a child, usually shows up at bedtime. When you have placed the child in his bed and the infant begin to cry, or if the child can talk. The child will ask you to leave his bedroom door open . . . . for the light to shine partially in his room.

Now, Parents, please do not feel offended when your child makes that request. Yes, you have created a safe environment for your child and *No, No, No* your child is not being a Wimp!! But something that day or week has temporarily traumatized your child or left a lasting empression in his or her mind.

What it could be?? Many events during a week or a day could have triggered this sudden insecurity in your child's mind. For example: The family could have been watching a T.V. movie together . . . when suddenly a commercial advertising a up and coming "Horror Movie" which is very scaary. As adults, you probably laughed at the commercial. But to a small child, that scary Movie commercial will replay itself . . . over and over in your child's mind. Each time your child thinks about that scary Movie, it becomes more a part of the child's realization in his thinking.

The same could be said about very violent images, such as those that are frequently shown on the Evening News. Scenes of War, Killings, and Deaths can really be detrimental to a child. Many of those horrifying images could stay with your child for several days. To most adults, we have been conditioned through the years, to view catastrophic images.

However, to a child, these images are very real. So, *Please, Please*, do not tease a child for being afraid. But, *Please*, be the understanding Parent who wants comfort the child. Through your Loving and Caring attitude, your child may find it easier to open up and express to you his fears. Stop for a moment and realize that we all have fears, whether conscious or subconscious. As adults, Parents, we all carry fears with us . . . . many of us have learned to suppress them over the years. For example: Some embarrassing or criminal thing we may have done in our so-called perfect childhoods . . . . that many of us try to sell to our children. God only knows that it would be nightmare if our children ever found out that mommy or daddy were involved in @#%¢@* when they were children. So Parents, give your child a break in this area of fears. Now, eventhough your child has told you about their fears . . . . TURN ON the Night Lite anyway.

A Nite-Lite is a very small investment to pay for temporary Peace of Mind. Remember, after a couple hours your child is asleep. You can quietly sneak back into the child's room and turn off the Nite Lite.

OTHER NITE LITE MOMENTS???

Always carry a Nite-Lite with you when you are traveling and your child is sleeping over night in a strange environment. For example in a hotel . . . . now the child can find his way to use the bathroom in the dark. Also, when you are visiting Grandmas' or your sisters' home. If and only if your child is sleeping in a separate room alone, use the Nite-lite. If the child awakes in the middle of the night, your child will be disoriented as to where they are. You will find that Nite-lites are mostly needed for a child sleeping alone. Usually, a child feels more safer if there is another child sleeping somewhere in that same room.

With younger children, you may want to keep a nite-lite ON IN THE bathroom. This may prevent a lot of clean up of Urine stains in the bathroom every morning. Children are rarely fully awake when they go to the bathroom at night. A Nite-lite in your bathroom will really help your child's night vision tremendously. In the bathroom, you can use a brighter bulb in the nite-lite

CHAPTER XVIII

WHY

YOUR

CHILD

IS

ATTRACTED

TO

CERTAIN

PEOPLE

WHY YOUR CHILD IS ATTRACTED
TO CERTAIN PEOPLE

Many people wonder why their children get involved with a wrong crowd. In other words, the child begins to hang out with peers of different upbringing. It is doubtful whether the child himself knows why he gets involved with the crowd, be it in search of love, acceptance, attention, self-esteem, or excitement. Whatever the reasons for troubles might be, if you as a parent are faced with this situation, contemplate this formula: the more time you spend with your child now, the less time you will spend getting your child out of trouble later on. This basic formula will work regardless of whether you understand or believe the intrinsic truth of it.

In the eyes of all young children, parents are their heroes, or role models. If only the parents would realize how awesome this time of their child's development is and take the advantage of these flourishing years to spend quality time getting to know each other. Yes, I did say, "getting to know each other." Parents, you must invest your time for your child to get to know you, their role models, as much as possible, and vise versa.

As you become more familiar with your child, you will realize that each child is born with unique attributes such as talents, temperament, and intelligence. Your child is born with certain gifts or talents that will enable him to develop his own niche in the world, regardless of whether your child's conception was an accident. Most people do not recognize the reality of these talents and they stroll through life oblivious to their natural gifts.

Some socioeconomic environments might even hinder people from exploring their inborn gifts, the reason for which a great number of high school graduates waste scholarships and their parents' finances in college "trying to find themselves." If you are an observant parent, by middle-school years your child should be participating in activities that would exercise his talents and gifts, be his interests sports or social clubs. This issue will be further discussed in greater detail in chapter "Career vs. Destiny."

If you have more than one child, you may note that your children may react differently to the same situations, or that a specific disciplining action might work with one child but not with the other. This difference is known as "temperament," which characterizes your child's behavior and personality: passive, hyperactive, or maybe just strong-willed. Your child's temperament is seen in his approach to every day problems, in the way he adapts or responds to any changes in the environment, and in his general mood. A great tip in parenting is to seek professional help to learn your child's temperament. Many hospitals, especially children hospitals, have qualified and very helpful child psychologists; in addition, you might want to research books on this subject of temperaments. Please, understand that this discussion is not in reference to astrological (Zodiac) personality traits.

Recognizing and acknowledging your child's temperament will ease your dealings with your child, meaning that you will not have as many rough moments. This knowledge will also help you in disciplining your child. Some young children may have to be scolded only once, others you might have to reprimand many more times. Some children may only have to *see* the "spoon of correction" to behave, to others you might have to *apply* it.

In this last paragraph, I would like to reiterate the importance of spending time with your children. As your children are still young, make an effort to be present in the play area during their interaction with other children. You will note the way children's role-play reflects their parents' behavior and upbringing. Through their play, children will reveal things they have been exposed to at home or at school. Silently continue observing the young ones and you will make some surprising discoveries about your own child.

CHAPTER XIX

SINGLE

PARENTHOOD

SINGLE PARENTHOOD

"Stability" is the key word in good child-upbringing. Parading different men through child's life will place the seed of insecurity within the young. Unfortunately, this condition exists in many single parent homes. A single mother will naturally seek a mate or a father figure for her children. Not all mothers seem to realize that not every man they meet is a good role model, or ready to settle down within an already-made family. Raising children single-handedly is challenging enough, the last thing a single mother would need is an overgrown delinquent to deal with.

If you are a single parent, delight in the years of raising your child the way that you feel is the best without unnecessary distractions. Do not go out of your way to look for a Mr. Right. Concentrating on doing the right thing for you and your children. As far as finding a role model for your male children, consider being more involved in the community. Expose yourself and your children to local churches, which are known for their focus on children development and growth. Some churches would have active youth activities, and generally would have mature, responsible youth leaders, rather than drug or alcohol addicted young adults. Research within your community about boys' & girls' clubs, YMCA, city parks, and Recreation Departments that are involved with youth activities and sports programs. If you as a parent have any arts background, perhaps you may wish for your child to become involved in youth theater or performing arts clubs.

Take some time to check with your area Chamber of Commerce, or Local Newspaper to research if any scandals or mishaps have been associated with any of these organizations. In many of these organizations the workers, such as coaches and leaders, are required to undergo a background check for past arrests or illegal activities. Before signing your child up for any of these clubs, you as a parent have the right to inquire into these background results. Take it seriously. As parents we always want to protect our children, limiting their exposure to crime.

Enjoy your single parenthood with your children. If you give your best to it, you can surely make your life joyful; you are in control of setting the atmosphere within your household. You can make your children happy or sad, delighted or depressed. I totally understand the difficulty of single parenthood and the responsibility of fulfilling both roles, but I also realize that we should beware of the feeling called "loneliness." To avoid loneliness, we would venture into some horrific relationships or new friendships that have no future.

To the single parents, take it to heart that you will probably meet a suitable partner when you least expect it, such as in the grocery store, or the post office. Meet this new person for a date in a very public place. Drive your own car, in case the date should end early due to improper behavior and you will find yourself in need to get away. Remember to get to know that person very well before inviting him to your home to meet your children. Wait for the time when you will be sure that this relationship will be safe and healthy to your children. When you are responsible for a life of a youngster, keep his or her future and well-being in mind. Children need stability, consistency, and security—so think it through on whether you would want to enter an unstable relationship that might uproot your children away from their familiar school, friends, and neighbors.

Be cautious when you decide on introducing your new adult friend to your children. Remember the innocence of children and their trust in their parents and the "friends" of their parents, for with the introduction you are presenting your acquaintance to your children as your "friend." If in the future, you will find yourself in need of disassociating from your newly-found friend, children in their naiveté would be very much confused by this change. There are evil people who love to enter fear-filled, controlling relationships. As a parent, you are and should always be in fear of your children's safety. Try to get to know your new friend without sexual contact as quickly as possible. Your friend should be willing to open up to you, if not beware of what that person might be hiding. Be strong and walk away from that relationship before it has developed into something serious.

As you keep your children in mind, remember not to enter a relationship with someone who does not want or like children. If he or she does not like them now, why would you suppose they would later on? Do not try to enter into a relationship with someone with a deep secret that you are aware of but he would not open up. Who knows if those secrets are not harmful to either you or your children? Many times, children can be good gauges in determining the relationships. For example, if your child feels uncomfortable in the presence of your new friend, listen to your child's instincts. Children in their naiveté and innocence are usually correct in judging an adult's character.

Remember, it is more important to have a safe home for yourself and your children, than a tension-filled household with an attractive male roommate.

CHAPTER XX

MEDIA

(RADIO, T.V.'S EFFECT)

MEDIA

In the times that we live today, I feel I must mention a few things for the benefits of a few readers or their friends. Today, our media, such as TV and radio, bombards us with shows reflecting immoral themes. These shows convey messages such as how acceptable and maybe even laudable it is to have a sexual relationship with any handsome young man who is financially stable. Let's be honest, is not the basic term for such behavior—"prostitution"? That Mr. Wealthy could have a bad temper, or grew up in an abused household, but the financial benefits of the relationship such as a diamond bracelet or a trip to Bermudas will compensate for bruises and destroyed self-esteem. Be careful of what you accept from media as "right" or "all-right," while in soap operas there are no "bad" endings, you cannot say the same about your life.

Allowing children to watch Violence on TV, video games, etc.

Many of today's Video games display explicit sex and violence. Please, do not feel that you are invading your child's privacy by sitting down with your child observe his movie or T.V. show. Also, observe your child playing video games with his friends. If your child asks, "why are you watching them play?" Just calmly respond, that they were sounding like they were having a lot of fun. "I need a *Fun Break*, cause what I was doing was so Boring!!" "So, thanks guys for letting me hang out with you". If your child seems agitated (uneasy), you arrived at a good time. Tell your child, "Oh, pretend that I am not here". The power of media can have a devastating effect on children. Teenagers will always tell you that they can handle it. With Teenagers, you must catch those opportunities to discuss the facts of life. If you are not embarrassed talking about sexual or drug related issues, neither are teenagers. If teenagers do not learn about Life from Mature level headed Parents, they will believe the *LIES* projected to them from Hollywood. Movies tend to glamourize Drugs and sex in a fascinating, yet distorted way, You, as a mature Parent, can set the record straight for them.

CHAPTER XXI

MONEY

WISE

(OR FOOLISH)

MONEY-WISE

Today's world is financially demanding; so many of us want so much more than we can afford. Who would not want the best for their children? better clothing? longer vacations? shorter working hours? We all see how difficult money-earning can be, especially through purely decent methods, and hence, too many people become enticed into the "easy gain-easy loss" ways. Money is rather fast in the criminal world, the influential trend of which is perceived in the trade of drugs and sex.

Selling sexuality is not a career for anyone regardless of circumstances, especially for a single parent, who is responsible for her child's life. What do these occupations convey to these children? That their mother does not respect herself or her body? These occupations bring more than shame to the children and the entire family. A dancer at a strip club exposes herself to people of low morals, and is in danger of being stalked and harmed. Stalkers are usually people with some psychological imbalances resulting in their abnormal behavior; would you really want such people to find out your home address? As a single mother take caution of how you dress and the message you might convey to males surrounding you. There is a defined line between stylish-sexy and sleazy-sexy. Too revealing clothes will attract attention of mentally unstable people regardless of the neighborhood you live in. Unfortunately, there are wolves walking around everywhere disguised in sheep clothing, even business suits.

The drug world industry is dictated by different laws, the resulting actions of which are not regarded as acceptable humane behaviors by outsiders. Would you really want these violent people to have problems with you and your children? Every day we see new faces of missing children on milk cartoons or online newspapers—children's own bedrooms are not safe anymore! I am not attempting to scare you into moving to an isolated place no one ever heard of, or putting up jail bars in your child's bedroom next to his oversized teddy bear, or acquiring a nun's habit to wear to work. I am just trying to arouse your sense of caution so you would be more conscious of the reality that might affect you and your children.

CHAPTER XXII

JUST

TWO

HOURS

A

WEEK

JUST TWO HOURS A WEEK!!!!

You will be amazed with all that can be accomplished in "JUST TWO HOURS A WEEK" There is one huge factor that makes all mankind equal, regardless of Race (color of skin), Ethnic culture, Educated or uneducated, Rich or Poor, Big or Little, Fast or Slow. That factor is "TIME". Fortunately, we are all given 24 hours in everyday. How we individually spend our 24 hours each day . . . will determine the difference of success or failure in our own lives, also for our children. I am always reminded of this Businessman's slogan, "The rich get richer while the poor watch T.V.". That slogan is made true everyday in our society with time management.

Despite the fact, that every single living person around us has been granted 24 hours a day, which is 168 hours in every week. It seems that no one has any time. BUT!!! If there is something that you really, really want to spend time doing. You will (miraculously) make the time or you will somehow find the time to do that thing (whatever it is).

Now, if you were to ask any Parent, of any child, "Would they want the best for their child???". They would all say "YES!!!" Again, if you were to ask those same parents, "Do you want your child to have better opportunies in life . . . than they had growing up???" Every single Parent would scream out loud, "YES, YES, YES!!!" Now, if you the reader of this chapter would also say "YES!!!" to those questions. Well, Let's get started giving our children a better education than we received.

First, let's start by scheduling two hours per week helping our children. For some Parents, this may suggest that we will have to turn off our televisions for those two hours a week (for our childs seek). We will spend those two hours either assisting our children or finding resources to help our children with their Schoolwork. If you are like me, I've been away from school over 25 years. Or maybe, you (as a parent) never finished school. For whatever reason (the reason does not matter), you dropped out of school. SO WHAT!!! You can be very useful with helping your child find resources to help him or her with their schoolwork. Remember, even when your child says that they have NO homework. Ask them to bring home the books of their most challenging subjects. You can help them to find supplemental resources to help them to understand what is being taught in the class. You can help your child before they fall behind in their classwork.

STOP!!!! I can hear many of you Parents saying to yourself "I don't have the time!!!". Well, let us do a little math problem to see if you really do not have the time (Just two hours a week) to give to your child better opportunies in life:

YOUR TIME SCHEDULE	PURPOSE OF YOUR TIME
40 Hrs/wk	Full time Job
25 Hrs/wk	Part-time Job (or overtime)
10 Hrs/wk	Commuting (Driving to Jobs)
52 Hrs/wk	Sleeping (7.5 Hrs/night)
17 Hrs/wk	Eating Meals (2.3 Hrs/day)
-144 Hrs/wk	Necessities of life (Job, sleep, food)
168 Hrs/wk (subtract)	Hours given to you each week
24 Hrs/wk	An entire day leftover to do whatever we
(Well, Look, Here!!!)	chose to do with it !!!!!

Well, Let's all be good Parents and chose to give "Just two hours a Week" to our children. You will still have 22 hours/wk to do with as you chose (golf, Ballgames, Soup Operas, the Gym). Just 2 hours is all that is needed to devote to assisting your child with creating a better life. Many Parents will plead ignorance when talking about their children's schoolwork. Let's see what we are really discussing here. Is it "IGNORANCE OR LAZINESS"??? Both can be overcome through a little afford and well power. First of all, there is no shame in being ignorant or uneducated in a subject matter. In the Modernized (computerized) subject matter that our children are using in the classrooms today. They are very intimidating, because they are very different than those in our school days. I am not ashamed to say, that when I went to school, the use of a calculator was a big deal. Also, we all have Strengths or Aptitudes. Some people have a natural gift in (for example) Mechanics, therefore you are an outstanding Handy-Man or working on Cars . . . sitting down and reading a book is very difficult for you. Or you may have a Social Aptitude, and you just love sitting down talking with any stranger needing conversation. Again we all have different strenghts, but do not allow that to stop you.

Now, let us start with a great resource for knowledge and education, "*The PUBLIC LIBRARY*". Do not fear, the Public Library is your friend. Please, look at the Public Library as a friendly source of information and services to the community. All of the Library's resources are "FREE"! To have a Library card for the whole family is totally free. It does not matter that you dropped out of school, because everyone at the library is seeking help to find information.

The Public Library is made possible by your hard earned Tax dollars. So, the library workers are paid to help you, your children, and everyone in your community. Many of the Public Libraries provide Free Internet usage, as well as, Books, Videos, Audio Books. That's right, if you cannot read, the library has Audio Books (which are Books being read on tapes). The Library provide Tapes and CD's with headphones. So you may sit quietly and look at the pages of a book while someone reads the book to you thru the tape machine. If you are blind parent or child, there is a section of the Library with Books in Braille. The Library workers will be happy to show you and your child helpful learning tools that can help all levels of school work. Parents, while your child is looking for helpful learning tools to take home (check out of the library), You can explore the Library's vast section of Music Tapes or CD's, or the Movie section of the Library. You can find Videos on every subject, for example: Gardening, Home Repairs, Auto Repairs, Cooking, Home Budgeting, etc., as well as, Entertainment Movies. Just Two Hours a Week in the local Public Library will bring amazing results for both you and your child at No Cost (other than your transportation getting there).

Another Resource of Educational Assistance for your child is the local Boys and Girls Club. Many Boys & Girls Clubs provide more than recreational Activities. Most Boys & Girls Clubs have College Intern Students working on their staff. These Intern Students are from nearby Colleges and Universities, working at the Club for College Credits.

Call the nearby College and ask to speak to a representative in their School of Education. You ask that Representative about Tutoring Programs That their Students are involved or provide in Primary or Secondary Education. These Students are studying to become Teachers. So, the School of Education has programs that their Students must go into the community as Student-Teachers to provide Teacher Assistance or Tutoring to schools for College Credits towards their graduation. So, your child may be able to be helped by one of these Future Teachers with his or her school Work.

Again, this is just another way that "Just Two Hours a Week" can benefit your child's development.

****** Of course, You, the Parent, must be present at the meeting place of your child's Tutoring Sessions. Be a wise Parent, never leave your child to go off alone to a meeting place with another Adult. *Student* or *Not* You still protect your child from uncomfortable situations. Preferably if possible, try to get a female Tutor for a female child, and a male Tutor for a male child.

Again, You the Parent should be present at all Tutoring Sessions You should be within listening distance at all times. In these Private Sessions, No matter if it is a Teacher, Teacher's Aide, or Student Tutor, You as the Parent must be *RESPONSIBLE*. We live in a Time where many RESPECTABLE PEOPLE do *NOT* always conduct themselves using *GOOD MORAL RESPECTABLE JUDGEMENT*!!!!! **************

CHAPTER XXIII

PARENTAL

PRESSURES

PARENTAL PRESSURES

Today, our children are faced with enormous amounts of peer Pressures. Every kind of Peer Challenges, such as: Popularity, Clothing trends, Fear Factors (dares, how far will you go), Sexual (Boyfriends, Girlfriends), drug related, etc. Today's Peer Pressures are far greater than any pressures of 10 to 25 years ago. So, the last thing that your child needs in his or her life is more pressure, especially Parental Pressures.

Parental Pressures can be as innocent as your child doing well in school. All Parents would like that their child do well in schoolwork. But there is a difference in encouraging your child to do well and demanding that your child bring home only A's and B's . . . . or there will be "HELL" to pay if they do not. Demanding that your child performs well or else . . . . just adds to their pressures.

Inside the Heart of every child is that special place where they desire to please their parents. Many others will say that each child seeks the acceptance or approval of their parents. You can all agree that since the birth of your child, your child has performed many different stunts to gain your attention . . . . Both positive and negative stunts have been attempted to gain your attention. Well, as your child grows that need for acceptance grows. Depending on where that child finds the most Love and acceptance. Of course, the perfect place for your child to receive the most Love and affection should be in his or her own home. Total acceptance from that child's own Family members. Unfortunately, many Homes (family members) place a "CONDITIONAL CLAUSE" for that Love and Acceptance. Usually, it is (1) If the child acts a certain way or (2) Achieves certain Goals (Live up to certain expectations). Many of these conditions begin very early in the child's Home life and they never experience Pure Love (Unconditional Love). That Love and acceptance just because you were born into that home, that family. Today, it seems like something dramatic will have to happen to that child before that child ever openly told about that PURE LOVE. It seems that a child has to be kidnapped or have to be involved in some horrible accident before a child's family will extend that Pure Love. The same mindset is that People never Pray for each other until they are faced with a Life threatening situation. Also, many children never see their Parents openly showing Love and Passion to one another outside of their Bedroom.

Well, all these loving mindsets should be the motivating factors when Parents ask certain chores from their child. Make should that your child knows that they are loved by you, whether they run the distance or fall down. Whether they receive an "A" or tried their best for a "C", they are loved by you. You, the Parent, understand that some subjects will be more difficult than others. Most children will not excel in all subjects in school. The teacher may not present the subject manner in a way that your child can comprehend.

In life there are many UPs' and DOWNs' and an abundance of choices in between. In a child's mind, they will base many of their choices on the values established in the home, also Love factors from their home environment. As proud Parents, we all desire more for our children than we recieved growing up. Please, Please be careful in this area, because this is usually where Parental Pressures begin. Those thoughts of our children growing up, only to continue the family legacy or continue the Family's Business. Having our children carry the Family Name on to greatness is almost every Parent's Dream. It is true that our children inherit our genes, but we must keep in mind that there are many environmental factors as well as Associational factors that made us into the personalities that we are.

For example: You, the Parent, may have a very successful LAW Career. You may be a tough, hard-nosed, dogmatic Attorney, who plans, strategizes, and you never lose a case. You grew up in the mean streets of New York City where you had to fight thru Street Gangs, just to get to school everyday. Plus, you grew up poor and you had to share a can of beans with five other Brothers, You had a life goal to get out of that environment and never go back. Yes, your environment made you tough and goal oriented. Now, STOP and THINK!!!! Your child is growing up in a totally different environment. their surroundings reflex the success that you have created for them. Your child lives in the soft, plush suburbs in a house. Their everyday challenge is a dirty school Bus in the mornings. They should not be expected to inherit your Drive and motivation towards your career and goals in life. Your children may not have the same aptitude or interest in the Legal Profession.

ANOTHER Example: Just because you (the Parent) were your Hometown All-American Quarterback in High School. That does not mean that your Son will be the same (chip off the old block). So, please, do not drag

your seven year old son down to PEE-WEE FOOTBALL tryouts to see what he is made out of. Your son may not show any interest in Sports until he is twelve or maybe never at all. If your son never plays a Sport in his Life. Please show him Love, Please Love him!! Possibly, he would rather be a Musician, play with Trucks, or just want to Build things. Still Love him for who he is becoming. With that Love, he will make you proud of him in some way.

Again, Please do not force your children to be like you or to have your same goals in their Lives. Allow them to develop into their own personality.

CHAPTER XXIV

DISARMING

THE

"ME"

CENTERED

TEEN

DISARMING THE "ME" CENTERED TEENAGERS

I sincerely hope that most of the readers do not have teenagers yet, but if you do this chapter might be helpful to you. We are all familiar with horror-like accounts of self-indulgent and self-oriented teenagers, no matter if they are our own or those of our neighbors. The means of disarming the self-centeredness of a teenager lays in these key words: "volunteering" time to some form of "community service."

Let us begin with parents of pre-teens or the children of the ages 10 to 12. As parents you must initiate the process of getting your pre-teen involved in volunteer work. Parents, take note of this advice for it will help you avoid future attitude problems from your potentially troublesome teenagers. There are numerous organizations that welcome volunteers of any age group: Boys' or Girls' clubs, functions for the Heart or Cancer Societies, or even Political Campaigns. Start out by inquiring around churches, hospitals, or retirement homes.

To initiate this rewarding process for your teenager, you as a parent perhaps will have to set up an example by getting involved with the volunteer work yourself. As an adult you can volunteer in the school districts or voting poles during local or national elections. Look at possible fun and beneficial things to do within your own community, such as different "Clean-up Campaigns." If you have difficulty finding a worthwhile community event, you may start one of your own and allow your children to help, working side by side with you. Perhaps, there is an old abandoned lot on your block that has been turned into a dump site—a rather unpleasant thing to have in your neighborhood. You can make that call to the City Hall to supply you with an empty container for trash; most city officials are very supportive of community clean-ups.

The lesson to be learned in participating in any voluntary work is to accomplish something out of self-less reasons, hence, shifting the focus from "my" to "others" needs. It is a marvelous occasion when teenagers begin to volunteer their time for greater needs or causes outside of their own.

CHAPTER XXV

CAREER

VS.

DESTINY

PART I

CAREER VS DESTINY PART I

"Career vs. Destiny" may very well be most effective chapter within this book regarding the future lifestyle of your child. This is a product of over 30 years of listening, learning, understanding life's challenges, and acquiring wisdom. Once again, I would like to emphasize that I in no way have the answers to all of life's questions; however, over the past 30 plus years, I have gathered enough experience and wisdom to help you in your quest to raise successful children.

Let us begin by defining career and destiny, both of which require hard work and dedication. A destiny is an act or course of life's action that results in an outcome that is internal and naturally predetermined. A career is the profession or occupation that a person chooses based on education, external motivation, and training. Unlike person's career, destiny is not chosen. Elements of person's destiny are to be found within that person's God-given talents and abilities. Developing and fine-tuning person's talents and abilities require exterior training and education.

Our colleges are filled with young students who are uncertain of their future occupations once they leave their halls of education. These students experiment with different career majors, basing their decisions on external information. It is well worth to remember the saying that opinions are like noses—everybody has one especially when it comes to giving an advice about future. Many helpful family members, friends, and even college advisors are quick to suggest their opinion of successful careers, usually based on monetary potential. However, these suggestions rarely consider personality, temperament, or inner desire of the individual person. Person's destiny is based on his inner drive and ability.

In children, desires and interests are two key elements in identifying areas of destiny. These elements begin to surface around the pre-teen ages lasting through teenage years. Some parents view this time of their child' development as a very challenging and difficult period. Let me assure you that it is no more challenging than turning the "terrible twos" into "tremendous threes." Keep in mind the formula I have given you in earlier chapters: the more quality time that you spend with your child the less time will you spend getting him out of trouble.

Many parents watch their children, but few observe them to discover their children's interest and natural God-given potentials. Observing interests and abilities require time and commitment on the part of the parent. It begins with a small step of noticing little things, such as whether your child enjoys working with numbers, or whether he prefers hearing literary stories. What stories interest him? Action? Drama? Does she act out the stories? Or, does he absorb it and retell it with colored pencils on a paper? What movies and television shows fascinate her? What is his favorite toy? Stuffed animals? Action figures? Simulated Automobiles? Computer games? Observe your child in interaction with other children. Is your child active or passive? friendly or confrontational? a leader or a follower, or maybe even both?

CHAPTER XXVI

CAREER

VS.

DESTINY

PART II

CAREER VS. DESTINY PART II

Trouble will find idle hands of pre-teens and teenagers; your child will be drawn to troublesome crowds if his time is not structured. In these young years, sports and other after-school activities are positive influences for teens. Encourage your children in their art or sports activities, like baseball, basketball, singing, instrument playing, or others. It is essential to have positive support and encouragement at home for the reason that many children do not reach their high potential due to negative atmosphere within their families. Take note of encouraging messages from T.V commercials such as "Be all you can be," or "Just do it!" The spoken word to children can either encourage or discourage them from their dreams.

Many fathers may not feel like attending their daughters' 1st grade plays. They would rather sit at home and watch the Monday Night pro Football Game. Think about it: there will always be another football game, but how many 1st grade plays would you see your daughter in as a little princess? Sacrifice watching the game, or better yet, record it, and go to support your daughter in her acting. She would be so happy to look out into the audience and see her Daddy smiling back positively. She would remember that fatherly support for the rest of her life. As she would get older, subconsciously she would seek a supportive boyfriend or a husband just like her father.

Allow me to share my personal child-rearing experience. I helped to raise four of my own children into adulthood. I wish I could say that as a parent I did everything right, handling every situation delicately and most efficiently, but in reality, no child comes with a manual, so I sought out wisdom from many grandparents. About twelve miles from our home was a self-help laundry facility that was set amid many homes in an established community of elders. Many of the neighborhood's elderly would gather every Saturday for the evening of laundry and, perhaps, a bit of gossiping.

I decided to make every Saturday night between 6:00 and 9:00 PM our family's laundry night. I would pack-up all of the laundry baskets and a mini-TV from the kitchen and off we would go to the Laundromat. I would set up the TV on a laundry table for my children to enjoy. While washers and dryers would be turning, I would wander over to the elderly. As I listened to their stories, I would make mental notes of different family situations and struggles, asking many questions about raising children. The elderly never failed to provide me with many different ways of handling any situation that might come up with my children.

My oldest daughter had a love for stories, especially animated ones, which she loved to share with her friends. For her birthday and Christmas, I made sure to gift her with stuffed animals and puppets. When she was in the 4th grade, during the parent teacher conference, her teacher and school counselor spent an hour trying to convince me that my daughter had mental disabilities due to her short attention span. I pulled my daughter out of that neighborhood elementary school and transferred her to a private school of higher scholastic standing, with a good arts and theater programs. New school's evaluation of my daughter was completely opposite; it rendered my daughter a genius status, advancing her to the next grade level. The evaluation was that she was bored in the previous school.

Later, we discovered that my daughter had filled up a couple of notebooks with short stories in her times of boredom. In high school, she won many writing awards. While in college she wrote a couple of plays, one of which the college performed publicly. During her college years, she was given the opportunity to work on a real Hollywood movie set of a produced film. Days after her college graduation, she was given immediate internship with one of three major television networks. She went on to become one of the Associate Producers of the #1 T.V show here in the US at the time. My daughter's college opportunity was a result of a small writing scholarship, but the majority was provided through athletic scholarships in tennis and volleyball. I made sure that all my children participated in sports and other after school extracurricular activities.

My second daughter at an early age acquired an affection for animals; she cherished the visits to the zoo. She was always occupied with a pet or two: rabbits, gerbils, fish, cats, and etc. As she was growing up, she was motivated by books and software involving zoology and biology. She was a wonderful student, maintaining excellent grades all through school, after which she received a full academic scholarship to a major university for veterinary medicine.

My youngest son was an impressionable child with a love for puppets and stuffed animals. He named each and every animal, making them talk. He could create an animated skit using stuffed animals as easily as breathing. I remember him putting on puppets shows for the neighborhood children. As a younger child, he was never interested in sports, but he loved movies and plays, so in his 6th grade year, I enrolled him into the Northwest Youth Theater Group. The Group concentrated on developing young actors by performing plays in local theaters. One day one of the instructors called me in for conference, informing me that my son had a special gift in entertainment.

He was very creative in theatrical techniques, amazingly holding attention of any audience. The theater recommended advancing my 6th grader to work with high school seniors; however, my son was intimidated performing with older teenagers.

For his 8th grade birthday, I gave my son a video camcorder. He was a natural behind a video camera. He would carry that camcorder everywhere, freezing many events in time. In high school, the Audio-visual Department instructor issued my son a key to the department office to be able to edit taping sessions for the school. Instructors advanced him to director/actor of school's audio-visual protects. After high school, my son went on to technical college for Camera Operation Technology. He was shortly promoted to number one in his class because of his natural gifts that his instructors immediately recognized. Class-work came easily to my son; he comprehended technology swiftly. At the present, he is on his way towards a scholarship for filmmakers school. No matter what area of entertainment or arts, my son's natural, or God-given, gifts would open doors of opportunity.

Encouraging your children towards their destiny will be challenging. Your child's gifting may be relating to future occupation that is not very popular or monetarily rewarding, but it is these many occupations and positions in life that keep this world functioning.

CHAPTER XXVII

WARNING

SIGNS

WARNING SIGNS

This is a very serious chapter called *WARNING SIGNS*. These signs or situations will require Professional Counseling to overcome. If you are experiencing any of these problems in your home, please talk with family Doctor for suggestions or a Church Minister that you may trust.

Let me start by saying, There is *NO SHAME* in the realization that you just *DO NOT KNOW WHAT TO DO* or the answer to a problem. Again, there is NO shame in not knowing. there are many things in Life that we just do not understand why it is. Especially, when it involves other human beings with somewhat normal intelligence. Unfortunately, children are not born with manuals on how they work. So, it is up to us to figure out and try to do the best that we can for our family. Sometimes, we need help. We, as Parents, must desire to find an answer that will improve our family's condition. So, we need to acknowledge that some situations require Professional help and counseling. Everyday, thru the News Media, we hear stories of child abuse and molestation, spousal abuses, and other types of weird problems found within the Family structure. These malfunctions can happen in any family regardless of Income status, Race, or other Cultural backgrounds.

The purpose of this Book is help you recognize possible problems, with insights that will help you towards healthy, happy children. Children that will be parts of Healthy, happy families. Again, I say that there are many situations that require the assistance of Professional Counseling. When I say Professional Counseling, I mean to seek the help of people who are Registered and Licensed with your STATE for Counseling in specified area of expertise. If you are part of a strongly religious family. Ask your Church office to refer you to only Registered Counselors, who are State Approved to Counsel. If your Church do not have State Registered Counselors on Staff, go to another Church that do or go to a state Agency. The reason you seek for Licensed or registered Counselors, is that by Law these Counselors are trained to recognize and notify the proper Law Enforcement Authorities if a criminal Offense has been committed. In many cases (such as battery—wife beating), it is very difficult to report a Boyfriend or other Family members who behave badly. State Registered Counselors must report Criminal Activities as a part of their Job. For example, if a family member is openly selling or using Drugs, in your home, around your children or abusively hurting your children.

(2) *WARNING SIGNS*

In this Millineum, there are media sources that carry and expose the general public to many immorally corrupt behaviors. Cable television and the Internet are two sources which are informational resources for just about anything (good or bad) imaginable. Many good people, who are family members and friends, develope secret appetittes for fetishes such as child Pornography. These fetishes are caused by the availability of the Internet or Massacistic desires from Adult Cable Channels. So please, please do not preassume that you can handle some of the following *warning signs*. I will now list a few situations which are warning signs for you to seek Professional help:

FOR LITTLE CHILDREN / INFANTS:

> **** It is difficult before they are able to talk, when they can talk

A) When your child begins to not want to talk; they clam up displaying some forms of fear or terror, while clutching tightly to some stuffed Animal. If this behavior continues over several days.

B) Your child's face shows FEAR, when you speak the name of a Babysitter or some other Adult who spends private time with this child. If your child speaks out "NO!!" when you say their Name. It does not matter who this person, family member, Boyfriend, Teenager from down the street or whoever.

C) Your child walks around physically handling their private parts, when they do not have to go to the Bathroom.

D) The child tries to touch your Personal private (Genital) areas.

E) When you extend your hand towards the child and the child flenchs (jumps back) from your hand.

F) The child runs or shows fear whenever you are handling certain items, such as: electrical cords, belts, stick-like items, cooking utensils, etc

CHILDREN OLDER THAN 6 YEARS OF AGE:

A) Your child comes to you to tell you that a certain Adult person has hurt them, or makes them hurt;

B) Your child mentions that they do not want to be around certain Adults whom they have had private moments.

C)   Your child begins to play with their stuffed animals in a sexual or violent type of way; trying to cut them.

D)   The child mentions about "Secrets" that they have with certain Adults that you know. The child cannot tell you about the Secrets;

WARNING SIGNS

E)   Your child displays fits of anger (rage) that is truely out of their character/personally.

F)   Your Live-in Boyfriend begins to hint to you to send your children away;

**** Remember, that at these ages children (even though they can talk may not be able to fully explain their feelings.

G) Your child begins to act withdrawn; obvious signs of timidity. They begin to distance themselves from other family members and friends.

MIDDLE / HIGH SCHOOL AGED CHILDREN

A)   When your teenager cuts off all communications or continually insists that you'll never understand. They begin a need for extreme Privacy; Locking their room all of the time and not allowing you to enter (never);

B)   When your teenager refuses to obey any of your requests, while blatantly displaying signs of irresponsibility; purposely disobeying curfews, etc. Total disrespect of Parental guidance.

C)   If you suspect Drug or alcohol use by your Teenager. Signs of drunkenness, loss of equilibrium, unusual extreme outbursts of insanity. Your Teenager begins friendships with questionable friends. Hanging out with Teens with criminal tract records. Bringing home strange paper bagged items, seemedly sneeking it into his room. Buying an abundance of air fresheners/ incenses.

D)   When your teenager is in the Bathroom, an unusual amount of the time or locked away in his room. When you walk by his room, you smell weird odors; such as the smell of burning rope, etc.

E)   When your teenager drastically changes his/her attire (the way that they dress). For example: Extreme or wild fashions. Like wearing all black with crazy tattooes and massacistic body piercings; or very scandally, provokative, sexually revealing clothing (showing lots of skin).

F)   Your teenager creates an appetite for violence or Satanic symbols and paraphemalia are found in his room; Posters on his wall depicting Death, violence or evil types of Horror.

**** The Teen is screaming out for attention . . . What Type???

CHAPTER XXVIII

HELPFUL

HINTS

(THE SUMMARY)

HELPFUL HINTS (SUMMARY)

I. *CREATE SAFE ENVIRONMENT* INSIDE THE HOME

A) CHILDPROOFING your home means to always think SAFETY first. Pending the age of the child, this may include padding sharp table edges, moving some electrical devices or breakables such as lamps, vases, or kitchen appliances. Also, keeping out of the sight and reach of children items such as: Household cleaning products, polishes, and other Poisonous substances. Sharp and pointed items, as well as items containing very small pieces that a child could put into his mouth.

**** Lock-up any and all Firearms or Weapons.

B) When purchasing gifts for smaller children, please make certain that these gifts are Age-Appropriate.

C) Provide proper lighting in Children play areas, television viewing rooms, study (reading) areas, or rooms for Computer usage. This will prevent Eye straining which could lead to vision problems later.

D) Monitor the Visitors that you bring into your home. A drunken (Alcoholic or Drug induced) Friend can have a long lasting negative effect on your young Impressional child. At first, they may seem harmless or even funny, but you will not want your child imitating these images.

E) When Bathing an Infant, remove or turn-off all distractions. For example: Turn off all cell phones or desk top phones, turn off all televisions, and turn off any items cooking (or on yoour stove). It only takes a few seconds for a child to slide under water. So, please do not leave until the bath is complete.

F) When you are cooking on the top of your stove, be sure to turn all pan handles to the inside of the stove. Out of the sight and the edge of the stove. Plug electrical outlets, cover exposed heating and gas valves, especially in older style homes or apartments.

****** The most effective way to childproof your home: Simply go into each room with a small stepstool. Sit on that stool and look around each room from your child's viewpoint, then remove (adjust) anything that might raise curiousity to your child.

II. *CREATE SAFE ENVIRONMENT* OUTSIDE THE HOME

A) Always make sure that your child is dressed appropriately when going outdoors to play, etc.

B) Examine your child's Play areas. Remove harmful items such as: Abandoned appliances (refrigerators, stoves, cabinets), old cars, big boxes (large plastic bags), broken glass, etc. Streets or parking lots with any amount of traffic are not safe play areas. Do not allow your child around swimming pools, lakes, or any form of ditch . . . nor exposure to a building site (construction site). You, as a parent, should always have a clear visible and accessible path to your child's play areas.

C) In the family car, make certain that all seat belts, doors, child car seats are in good working condition. Explain to your child, the dangers of playing with the door handles while the car is moving.

D) Teach your child about talking to strangers; especially helping a stranger find his lost puppy. This is very important, especially while playing or waiting for the School Bus. Take a few minutes to meet the School Bus Drivers who transport your children.

III. *MAKE SURE YOUR CHILDREN ARE SUPERVISED*

A) The Choice of a good Babysitter is to find the most responsible sitter. Most Community Centers and some School Districts offer courses in Babysitting for Teenagers. You will find that the best Teenage Babysitters have already taken one of these courses. Interview the Babysitter and also speak with their parents. Usually, the Teenager with the most home responsibilities make the best Sitters. For example: Teenagers with other siblings (Brothers and Sisters) living at Home. When Interviewing, Always ask about their Internet usage. Be very careful and do not hire an Internet Chat Line Junkie. Also Parents, be aware, that you do not become an Internet Chat Line Parent. In other words, you spend more attention to the Computer Conversations than your child.

   ****** Unfornately, Child Pornography is on the rise. Please, do not allow Teenagers or any outside Adult to take *NUDE* nor *PARTIALLY NUDE* Photographs of your children. *NO MATTER WHAT*, how innocent it might seem. Do not allow outside family (Uncles, Aunts, nephews, etc) members to Bath your children. You do the Cleaning of your children until they are a responsible Age.

B)   Never allow a slightly older child to watch another younger child without Adult Supervision somewhere on the premises (area).

****** Children will always act like Children.

C)   KNOW WHERE YOUR CHILD IS AT ALL TIMES; Know who your child's Friends are and where they live. If your child is ever invited to a Neighbor's Home for an overnight SLEEPOVER; you make sure that there will be responsible Adult supervision present all night. Sometimes, really weird AND BIZARRE SITUATIONS OCCUR in some neighborhood homes. Make a call, to guarantee that nothing out of the ordinary is happening there.

D)   NEVER, NEVER Leave a child in a Car with the Motor running. Too many things can go wrong. Having a licensed driving Adult in the car with the child is always the best. An Adult who drives can better detect an automotive malfunction, such as: Exhaust Fumes inside the car or the Engine= running Hot. Also, consider the outside Weather Temperature. If hot leave a window open or other air conditioning provisions for the car's occupants. If cold, proper heating necessary.

E)   Teach your children to never take pills or any Prescription Medications, without a Parent or responsible Adult present. Hopefully, that Adult is literate and capable of reading labels.

F)   Explain to your children the dangers of running thru store parking lots of any size. It is difficult for the Big Cars to see Little children. This leads to "*NEVER PLAY IN THE STREETS*". As explained in previous chapters, the importance of your child obeying your commands to "*STOP*". It could one day save their little life. That is why it is essential that you arrange for your younger children to be accompanied to the School Bus Stop. Especially, if there is traffic on that street. Your involvement in your child's life is always needed, especially if your child has special needs. Make the time, find the time, create the time to read books, play games, and tell stories to that special child of yours.

G)   Be aware of your physical location when playing with your younger children. A child (unaware of danger) will always think that it is cool (fun) whenever Dad tosses him up in the Air and catches him. But DAD, you must be aware of your playful location. An example: a balcony ledge, a deep body of water, or any place where your child could experience harm or injury if the child somehow (accidentily) slips thru your hands. Where could that child possibly land.

*** One of the most scariest moments of my parenting life was: one day, my wife was changing my son's diaper on the kitchen counter. She turned away for only four seconds to reach another diaper on the kitchen table. In a split second, my infant Son rolled off the kitchen counter . . . three feet onto the kitchen floor. Our hearts literally stopped beating . . .

Thank goodness for the very thick rug next to the counter where our son landed on the meaty part of his Buttocks. Our son was alright, but that could have been a tradgic situation for us.

IV. When your children begin school, take the time to get to know your children's Teachers. Create an open dialogue with their Teachers, So the Teacher feels comfortable calling you first, if there ever is a problem. Attend all PARENT-TEACHER CONFERENCES at their school. Periodically, check with the Teacher for a status report of your child's progress. All children will hide a bad grade or a bad school situation. Be aware of the things that your child is being exposed to at school. Know that you as a parent, have a right to write to the school and not allow your child to participate or be exposed to certain teachings or guest speakers. For example: Sex Education, Sexual Preference Training, crazy spiritual rituals, etc.

****** You don't want your child howling and chanting VOODOO!!! Or your child thinking that they were born a Vampire because they desire to eat red meat???

V. Never allow a child's opinion to overrule a Parent's decision. As they get older, children will allows challenge a parent's decision. Praise your child for making good choices in life and his good behavior. This is called, "Positive Reinforcement". But alos discuss with your child and punish bad behavior (behavior that is harmful to others) which may include: Time-outs, grounding, taking away priviledges. During your Family Time, discuss with your children about ways to handle Peer pressure problems appropriately. Different reactionary methods when faced with Insults, Threats, Drugs, or Unwanted Sexual advances. Prepare your

child to function in our tough, cruel, World. They will be strong if you
are strong in discussing those everyday challenges of life.

***** Remember, Parents raise the children, not the children raise
the Parent. So, be the Parent who stays in control of the home.

WITH THE CHILDREN THERE IS NO END

THIS IS JUST THE LAST PAGE

"ALWAYS, ALWAYS REMEMBER

******

"YOUR CHILDREN MAY BE OUT
OF YOUR HOME....BUT
THEY WILL NEVER BE COMPLETELY
OUT OF YOUR POCKETS"

******